One Pan, Two Plates

Vegetarian Suppers

One Pan, Two Plates
Vegetarian Suppers

MORE THAN 70 WEEKNIGHT
MEALS FOR TWO

Carla Snyder

PHOTOGRAPHS BY **Jody Horton**

CHRONICLE BOOKS

SAN FRANCISCO

Text copyright © 2016 by *Carla Snyder*.
Photographs copyright © 2016 by *Jody Horton*.

Library of Congress Cataloging-in-Publication Data:
Names: Snyder, Carla, author. | Horton, Jody.
Title: One pan, two plates : vegetarian suppers : more than 70 weeknight
    meals for two / Carla Snyder ; photographs by Jody Horton.
Description: San Francisco : Chronicle Books, [2016] | Includes index.
Identifiers: LCCN 2015039846 | ISBN 9781452145839 (pbk. : alk. paper)
Subjects: LCSH: Vegetarian cooking. | Suppers. | LCGFT: Cookbooks.
Classification: LCC TX837 .S6755 2016 | DDC 641.5/636—dc23 LC
    record available at http://lccn.loc.gov/2015039846

Manufactured in China

Designed and illustrated by *Cat Grishaver*
Chronicle books and gifts are available at special
quantity discounts to corporations, professional
associations, literacy programs, and other organiza-
tions. For details and discount information, please
contact our premiums department at corporate
sales@chroniclebooks.com or at 1-800-759-0190.

10 9 8 7 6 5 4 3 2 1

Chronicle Books LLC
680 Second Street
San Francisco, California 94107
www.chroniclebooks.com

To all the time-starved souls

WHO LIKE TO COOK, LOVE TO EAT,
BUT HATE TO WASH DISHES.

contents

CHAPTER 5
Pasta for Dinner

CHAPTER 6
Pizzas, Tarts, Tartines & Piadinas

At the end of a workday, our minds turn to all the things that need to be done upon our return home—cleaning, laundry, bills, e-mail, and the everyday chore of making dinner. I can't help you with your laundry or bills, but my book *One Pan, Two Plates: More Than 70 Complete Weeknight Meals for Two* has helped thousands to get made-from-scratch meals on the table with minimal time and less cleanup. The original book is full of meals with poultry, meat, and fish, and a smattering of vegetarian dishes—all of which are scaled for two people. Over the last few years, readers have clamored for more one-pan vegetarian dishes, and so *One Pan, Two Plates: Vegetarian Suppers* was conceived.

Our diets are changing, and fast.
Although only 5 percent of Americans define themselves as vegan or vegetarian and 6 percent of the British population responded similarly in a Mintel survey, almost everyone believes they need to eat better. But what does "better" mean? Most of us are trying to eat diets that are lower in processed foods, with fewer animal products and more veggies and whole grains. Whether you want to lower your cholesterol and blood pressure, lose weight, save money, or lessen the negative environmental effects of factory farms, eating less meat is something people of all ages are embracing.

That's where *One Pan, Two Plates: Vegetarian Suppers* comes in. This is a book for omnivores who would like to embrace a diet with less meat and more wholesome, delicious vegetables and grains.

Many of us are adopting the label *flexitarian*, which was originally applied to those who ate mostly vegetables, but also incorporated meat or fish into their diets. Flexitarians might be people who are moving their meat-based menus in a more vegetarian direction, or they might be vegetarians who are adding meat or fish back into their diets. The word *flexitarian* suggests a regimen that includes more whole grains, legumes, fruits, and vegetables than the standard diet. Flexitarians are not eliminating meat entirely but may want to eat more humanely raised meat, which costs more, so they are eating less of it.

The recipes you'll find here are for moderate, conscious eaters who don't want to adopt a drastic change in their diets, but who want to eat less meat. Though there is a plethora of vegetarian cookbooks available, most omnivores find them to be confusing and full of unfamiliar ingredients. Many of these people don't identify with vegetarianism or want to be vegetarians, they just want to eat a little less meat and need a road map to that end. *One Pan, Two Plates: Vegetarian Suppers* is a guide to smart, thoughtful, contemporary cooking and eating. I see it as a companion to my previous book, for those meatless nights we increasingly adopt per week.

This book isn't about a diet, but about a way of life that includes eating delicious meatless meals of satisfying food. From twenty-somethings to empty nesters, the public has changed their meat consumption habits for health and economic reasons. But eating more healthful meals can still be quick and easy. The seventy-plus recipes included here give you the information you need to feed your two-person household, quickly and deliciously, with just one pan to clean up.

The book has six chapters: Warming Soups & Stews is full of hot bowls, often with a warm sandwich on the side. Recipes like Moroccan Chickpea Stew with Harissa and Naan or Cream of Tomato Bisque with Toasted Cheddar and Apple Sandwich are simple to make as well as satisfying. The Eggs & Cheese, Please chapter features numerous frittatas and international dishes like

Bibimbap with Fried Egg, Shakshuka with New Potatoes, and Huevos Rancheros with Black Beans, while Garden-Fresh Dinners is a farmers' market of colorful, hearty meals like Fried Eggplant Stacks with Buffalo Mozzarella, Chermoula, and Pine Nuts and Roasted Brussels Sprouts with Butternut Squash, Apple, and Walnuts. The extensive Grains & Beans with Soul chapter is chock-full of good-for-you dishes such as Spiced Green Lentils with Sweet Potato and Pistachios and Crunchy Black Bean Tacos with Corn and Queso Fresco. The ten recipes in the Pasta for Dinner chapter don't disappoint, including Spinach Gnudi with Cabbage and Browned Butter as well as Linguine with Ricotta, Zucchini, Sun-Dried Tomato, and Lemon. The chapter titled Pizzas, Tarts, Tartines & Piadinas includes recipes for four different pizzas along with a gorgeous Root Vegetable Tarte Tatin and stunning Portobello and Beemster Piadina.

10

I wrote this book because I saw the need for a collection of easy-to-make vegetable-based weeknight meals for two from the viewpoint of an omnivore. I still eat meat and fish and think that most of you do as well. I am put off by faux food and most restrictive diets, and I encourage my students and readers to cook and eat a variety of foods, not only for good health but for the sake of interesting meals. These recipes prove that an enticing meal doesn't have to include meat in the middle of the plate. With all the flavorful vegetables, grains, pastas, egg dishes, soups, and stews included here, you won't become bored and you won't miss meat either. Inside these pages is an ethnic wonderland of meatless meals that will take you from Asia to the Middle East, Europe, and back to the Americas. I hope you enjoy the trip.

tips to help you cook with speed and success

Read the recipe before you turn on the stove. This is my Number One rule of the road. It's okay to preheat the oven before you read the recipe (the oven needs that time to get to the proper temperature), but it's important to get the lay of the land and know how you're going to proceed before you begin to cook. Pull all the ingredients from the fridge and pantry and arrange them on the counter. Take a moment to look through the recipe's instructions and then plan how you will begin the prep. Oftentimes, onions can sauté while you slice a carrot or mince garlic to add later in the cooking process. After all, we want to make dinner efficiently and smoothly, with less stress and more fun.

Learn to love your skillet. Many recipes in the book call for a 12-in [30.5-cm] skillet. For the best results, use a heavy skillet, such as one made from cast iron. Just cook with that heavy skillet for one week and you'll understand why they're so popular with serious cooks. A heavy skillet will allow you to use higher heat (which cooks food faster), resulting in a better sear and browned exterior than most lightweight cookware. I recommend a skillet with a lid and an oven-safe handle so that it can go from stove top to oven safely.

Have a deeper vessel to cook things like pasta, soups, and stews. A 3-qt [2.8-L] saucepan is the second-most-used pan in my house, and it will be in your home as well.

A heavy sheet pan will change your life. A sheet pan isn't a cookie sheet (though it can be used as one). It has sides, and the dimensions are usually 18 by 13 in [46 by 33 cm]. Don't buy the ones sold at the grocery store as they will warp in the oven as they heat up. Instead, opt for the heavier sheet pans that are sold in cookware stores. They'll hold up longer and perform at a much higher level.

Invest in a good knife and a honing steel. Cutting up vegetables with a dull knife is a chore, but a sharp knife makes cutting a pile of vegetables less work. I recommend a 7-in [17-cm] or 8-in [20-cm] santoku knife, which is a Japanese version of the traditional classic European chef's knife. Or, if you have chef-like aspirations, purchase a 10-in [25-cm] classic chef's knife. Once you get used to it, the extended length makes chopping easier and more fun. Whichever knife you choose, always rinse and dry by hand and never put it in the dishwasher, as the heat tends to dull the blade. The honing steel actually keeps your knife edge straight so that it doesn't have to be professionally sharpened more than once a year or so. (I take mine to our local farmers' market, where a professional will sharpen my knives while I shop.) Ask the salesperson to demonstrate how to bring a sharp edge back to your knife, or check out the technique online.

Purchase a large cutting board.
A large cutting board will give you plenty of room to cut all your fresh vegetables, and if it's plastic or wood composite, it can be washed in the dishwasher as well. Make sure to dry your cutting board thoroughly before putting it away, as it can mildew if it's stored damp.

Pay attention to how you cut your veggies.
Now that you have a good knife and a cutting board, you can easily follow the recipes in this book, which direct you to cut the vegetables a certain way for optimal cooking times and aesthetics. Make the cuts according to the recipe and your dinner will be on the table in no time flat.

Choose recipes using vegetables that are in season.
Though you can get just about any vegetable at any time of year, try to source locally grown vegetables as much as possible. They'll taste the best, and sometimes they're even cheaper than produce trucked in from halfway across the country.

Use a Microplane for zesting citrus.
I like how this tool allows you to utilize the intense flavor in the skin of lemons, oranges, and limes. Inexpensive and very useful, a Microplane will also effortlessly grate nutmeg and hard cheeses, such as Parmesan, like a pro. For the best results, zest citrus first and then juice it.

Keep an assortment of grains and legumes in your pantry at all times.
Grains and legumes figure prominently in this book, and they keep for lengthy periods of time. You'll definitely want long-grain rice, Arborio rice, farro, barley, lentils, bulgur, and quinoa, but other grains, like millet, einkorn, and wild rice blends, add variety and are fun to try as well.

Stock canned beans and tomatoes.
When you have these at the ready in your pantry, you're halfway to dinner. Always keep canned diced tomatoes and an assortment of canned beans, such as cannellini, black beans, chickpeas, and kidney beans, on hand for the unplanned dinners you cook on the fly.

Buy a box of kosher salt. Keep salt in a little bowl beside the stove so that you can grab it with your fingers and add it to your vegetables. The clean flavor of kosher salt is vastly superior to iodized salt, which can add a metallic taste to food. And don't be shy with the salt. You are cooking fresh food and, for the best flavor, it needs to be seasoned.

Freshly ground black pepper is more robust than packaged ground pepper. To give your food more oomph, buy a pepper mill (it needn't be expensive), fill it up with whole black peppercorns (I like Tellicherry peppercorns best), and grind the pepper directly onto your food while it's still cooking. Even if you don't like the heat of black pepper, a sprinkling of it will liven up your dish with ease.

Ethnic ingredients inject food with interesting flavors. It's fun to try new tastes, and it keeps the dinner table fresh and exciting. The few ethnic spices in the book are used in multiple recipes, so you should be able to use them up over time. Take a cruise down the international aisle at your grocery store or, better yet, seek out ethnic markets where

you can buy these new staples on the cheap. If you can't find the ingredients locally, stock up online.

Olive oil is a healthful option for cooking. The general rule is to use extra-virgin olive oil, which is more expensive, for salads and uncooked foods and regular olive oil and vegetable oil for cooking. I prefer expeller-pressed vegetable oils that are processed without extra chemicals or heat, making them a more healthful option.

Vegetable broth adds intensity to foods. Sometimes I use vegetable broth instead of water for extra flavor when cooking rice or legumes. The best way to buy it is in an aseptic or cardboard container. Just use what you need, close the spout, and store it in the fridge for up to a week. It will be ready and waiting for the next time you want your dish to have more depth.

Buy the onions in the 3-lb [1.4-kg] mesh bag. There aren't many recipes in this book that don't start with a tasty onion. When cooking for two, those bagged onions are just about the right size.

Fresh garlic is a must. A bulb will keep for weeks in a bowl on your counter. Garlic preferences are personal, so if the cloves are small and you like a lot of garlic, add another clove. Likewise, if the cloves are large and the recipe calls for two, one may be enough.

Shallots rock. Shallots are like baby red onions. They are mild, sweet, and perfect to use raw for flavoring vinaigrettes or to cook up with mushrooms or other lightly sautéed vegetables. Store them with the garlic on your counter.

Collect an assortment of vinegars. Like spices, vinegars add nuance to food. You'll definitely want to have rice vinegar, balsamic vinegar, cider vinegar, and white wine vinegar in the pantry, but others, like sherry, Champagne, and flavored vinegars, can be subbed in for extra interest as well.

Hot sauces aren't just for pepper heads. Stock up on chile-garlic sauce, Sriracha, Louisiana Hot Sauce, Cholula, or whatever hot sauce appeals to you. Just a dash will add nuance to your dinner. A few dashes will add heat if you like it hot.

Never underestimate the power of the egg. Eggs are one of the best fallback dinner ingredients. If you have eggs, you have a potential dinner. If you have some grated cheese, even better.

Make the most of frozen rice for extending meals. My grocery store sells it (both white and brown) in microwavable bags. I nuke it for 3 minutes, and it's ready to go.

Serve meals on heated plates. Heat plates (with no metal decorations) in the microwave for about 1 1/2 minutes just prior to serving dinner. It's amazing how much longer your food will stay hot on the plate, allowing you to linger at the table and discuss the events of the day.

If your oven has a convection setting, you're crazy not to use it. Convection cooking uses hot air to roast and bake. Foods brown and caramelize faster in convection mode, and your oven will preheat faster as well. To adapt these quick-cooking recipes to convection mode, just set your oven temperature as directed in the recipe and set the timer a few minutes less. Monitor the food for doneness until you get the hang of convection cooking.

15

CHAPTER

1

Warming Soups & Stews

Cream of Tomato Bisque

with TOASTED CHEDDAR and APPLE SANDWICH

As a nod to your six-year-old self, creamy tomato soup with a toasted, cheesy sandwich is a heavenly meal when you need a little weeknight pampering. Few would deny the charmed memory of Campbell's tomato soup and mom's toasted Velveeta-stuffed Wonder bread (triple-brand callout alert), but somehow this grown-up version is, um, *waaaaay* more delish. Better cheese and bread and a crispy apple elevate the sandwich, and a little wine spikes the soup. Mom would definitely approve.

4 slices sourdough bread

2 Tbsp mayonnaise

2 Tbsp grainy Dijon mustard

Thin slices from 1 crisp apple such as Braeburn, Honeycrisp, or Gala

2 oz [55 g] sharp Cheddar cheese, thinly sliced

2 Tbsp olive oil

1 small onion, diced

1 garlic clove, minced

½ tsp dried basil

½ tsp dried oregano

¼ cup [60 ml] white wine

Two 15-oz [425-g] cans crushed tomatoes

1 cup [240 ml] vegetable broth

½ cup [120 ml] half-and-half

Kosher salt and freshly ground black pepper

2 Tbsp minced fresh flat-leaf parsley

1. Spread one side of each slice of bread with the mayonnaise. Lay two of the slices mayo-side down, spread with the mustard, and lay several slices of apple and then the cheese on top. Cover the cheese with the remaining bread slices, mayo-side up.

2. Heat a 12-in [30.5-cm] skillet over medium-high heat, and cook the sandwiches until browned on both sides, about 3 minutes. Transfer the sandwiches to a plate and keep warm.

3. Add the olive oil to the pan. When the oil shimmers, add the onion, garlic, basil, and oregano and sauté until the onion softens, about 3 minutes. Add the wine and cook until it almost completely evaporates, about 3 minutes. Add the tomatoes and vegetable broth and bring to a simmer. Turn the heat to low and simmer until the flavors have blended, about 5 minutes. Stir in the half-and-half and taste for seasoning, adding salt and pepper, if it needs it.

4. Ladle the soup into heated bowls and sprinkle with the parsley. If you like, cut the sandwiches into "fingers" so they are easily dipped into the soup. Serve hot.

It's that easy: An immersion blender is a super-handy tool. If you have one, use it to blend the soup until it's smooth and then toss the business end of it into the dishwasher for easy cleanup.

Extra hungry? Make an extra sandwich.

In the glass: This updated classic needs an adult beverage. Try a Blue Moon Belgian pale ale.

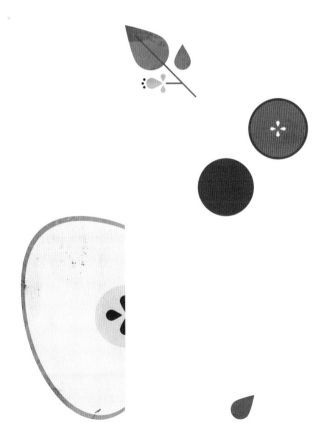

Cheesy Cream of Cauliflower Soup

with LEEK and RYE CROUTONS

Cauliflower makes one of the most delicious soups. And it's packed with vitamin C and dietary fiber, so it's not only great tasting but good for you too. Rich and creamy with just enough Cheddar cheese to make it seem decadent, this is the stuff that comforts and soothes at the end of a hard day.

3 Tbsp unsalted butter

2 slices rye bread, cut into cubes

1 leek, white part only, cleaned and thinly sliced

1 stalk celery, diced

½ head cauliflower, trimmed and finely chopped

½ tsp fennel seeds

Kosher salt

2 cups [480 ml] vegetable broth

½ cup [120 ml] half-and-half

2 Tbsp all-purpose flour

½ cup [40 g] grated Cheddar cheese, plus more for garnish

A few drops fresh lemon juice

Pinch of cayenne pepper

Freshly ground black pepper

Minced fresh chives for garnish

1. Heat a 12-in [30.5-cm] skillet over medium-high heat, and melt 1 Tbsp of the butter. Add the bread cubes and cook until browned and crispy, about 4 minutes. Transfer the croutons to a plate.

2. Add the remaining 2 Tbsp butter to the pan along with the leek, celery, cauliflower, fennel seeds, and ½ tsp salt. Cook the vegetables, tossing often, until they begin to soften, about 4 minutes; be careful not to let the bottom of the pan overbrown.

3. Add the vegetable broth and half-and-half and bring to a simmer. Turn the heat to low and simmer until the cauliflower is tender, about 10 minutes.

4. Meanwhile, in a small bowl, toss the flour with the cheese.

5. When the cauliflower is tender, turn the heat to medium-high and whisk the cheese-flour mixture, a little at a time, into the soup to thicken it. Let the soup bubble for a minute, then add the lemon juice and cayenne and season with salt and black pepper.

6. Ladle the soup into heated bowls. Garnish with the croutons and sprinkle with cheese and chives. Serve hot.

It's that easy: *Tossing the cheese with flour helps the cheese to assimilate into the soup while also thickening it. If you want the soup to be white, just use aged white Cheddar.*

Extra hungry? *Drizzle a few additional slices of rye with olive oil and toast them in the toaster. Lay them at the bottom of the heated bowls and ladle the soup over the top. They'll soften in the soup but still be nice and chewy.*

In the glass: *A buttery Chardonnay from Edna Valley would be a fine choice here.*

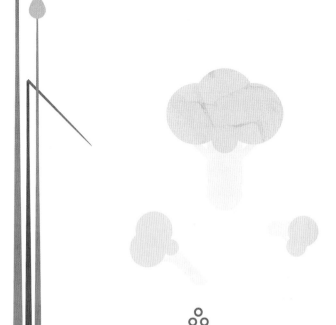

....
START TO FINISH
30 minutes
...
HANDS-ON TIME
20 minutes
...
Serves 2
....

Avgolemono Soup

with GREEK SALAD

Nothing could be simpler than this classic soup, rich with eggs and bright with lemon. My dad loved this dish and used to eat it for lunch every day at the little luncheonette, People's, down the street from his place of business. I remember WPA murals on the walls, a long counter, and a few tables always filled with steelworkers on break from the mill across the street. Dad also couldn't resist a fresh Greek salad on the side (I like to prepare it while the soup cooks). This one's for you, Dad.

Avgolemono Soup

4 cups [960 ml] vegetable broth

¼ cup [55 g] long-grain rice

2 eggs

3 Tbsp fresh lemon juice

Kosher salt and freshly ground black pepper

Greek Salad

2 Tbsp red wine vinegar

1 garlic clove, minced

Kosher salt and freshly ground black pepper

1 tsp Dijon mustard

Leaves from 1 sprig fresh oregano, minced

¼ cup [60 ml] extra-virgin olive oil

½ small cucumber, peeled, seeded, and cut into ½-in [12-mm] slices

1 tomato, cut into about 8 wedges

¼ red onion, cut thinly into rings

¼ cup [30 g] crumbled feta cheese

8 pitted Kalamata olives

1. To make the soup: In a 3-qt [2.8-L] saucepan over medium-high heat, bring the vegetable broth to a simmer and add the rice. Turn the heat to low, cover, and gently simmer until the rice is almost tender, about 15 minutes. Turn off the heat, uncover, and let sit until the mixture cools, about 10 minutes.

2. In a large heat-proof bowl, whisk the eggs and then add 2 cups [480 ml] of the warm broth and rice in a thin stream, whisking constantly. Quickly transfer the egg mixture to the soup in the pan, whisking constantly so that the eggs don't curdle but the soup still thickens slightly. Add the lemon juice and season with salt and pepper. Cover and keep warm.

3. To make the salad: In a large bowl, combine the vinegar, garlic, a pinch of salt, and a few grinds of pepper. Let the mixture sit until the flavors blend, about 5 minutes. Whisk in the mustard and oregano. Pour the olive oil into the vinegar mixture in a thin stream, whisking constantly until an emulsion forms. Add the cucumber, tomato, onion, cheese, and olives to the bowl and toss to coat with the dressing.

4. Ladle the soup into heated bowls and serve with the salad on the side.

It's that easy: For a soup this simple, use the best broth you can buy. Organic varieties usually taste better and contain less salt. Look for broth in the aseptic (cardboard) box since you can refrigerate the unused broth directly in the container.

Extra hungry? It's easy to add toasted bread to the salad. I keep a bag of crostini chips in my pantry for just such an occasion. Crumble them over the top to make the salad a little more filling and to add a little crunch.

In the glass: The soup and salad are tart, so I'd go for an iced tea with a slice of lemon, sweetened or not.

Chunky White Bean Soup

with GREEN BEANS and ROSEMARY-GARLIC CROUTONS

When I'm looking for a fast and fresh dinner, I look to soups like this one, which is chock-full of creamy canned beans but with a dose of fresh green beans to make it more appealing and colorful. Rosemary-garlic croutons round out this bowl so that it's a complete meal; but let's face it, garlicky toasted bread could make just about anything taste delicious.

2 Tbsp olive oil, plus more for drizzling

1 onion, diced

2 garlic cloves; 1 minced, 1 peeled

1 carrot, thinly sliced

$\frac{1}{2}$ stalk celery, thinly sliced

1 tsp dried basil

Kosher salt and freshly ground black pepper

One 15-oz [425-g] can cannellini beans, drained

2$\frac{1}{2}$ cups [600 ml] vegetable broth

3 new potatoes, thinly sliced

4 oz [115 g] green beans, trimmed and cut into bite-size pieces

1 tsp honey

$\frac{1}{2}$ tsp white wine vinegar

2 slices country-style bread

2 tsp minced fresh rosemary

Shaved Parmesan cheese for garnish

1. Heat a 3-qt [2.8-L] saucepan over medium-high heat, and add the olive oil. When the oil shimmers, add the onion, minced garlic, carrot, celery, basil, $\frac{1}{2}$ tsp salt, and a few grinds of pepper. Sauté until the vegetables begin to soften, about 3 minutes.

2. Add the cannellini beans, vegetable broth, and potatoes to the pan and bring to a simmer. Turn the heat to low and simmer until the potatoes are tender, about 10 minutes. Add the green beans and simmer until the beans are tender, about 5 minutes longer. Stir in the honey and vinegar. Taste and season with more salt or pepper, if it needs it.

3. Meanwhile, drizzle one side of the bread slices with olive oil and toast in a toaster. When crispy and browned, remove them from the toaster and rub the peeled garlic clove over the oily side of each and sprinkle with the rosemary.

4. Lay the toast in the bottom of heated bowls and ladle the soup over the top. Garnish with shaved Parmesan. Serve hot.

It's that easy: *If you don't have fresh green beans, go ahead and use frozen ones. You can also add some peas, corn, or lima beans if you feel like cleaning out the freezer.*

Extra hungry? *Add a few more potatoes and another ¹/₂ cup [120 ml] broth to the soup. Or if you have an opened box of pasta, ¹/₂ cup [55 g] of penne, shells, or rotini will be sure to fill you up.*

In the glass: *Zinfandel is a rich, jammy wine. Look for a bottle of Kunde Estate Zinfandel from Sonoma.*

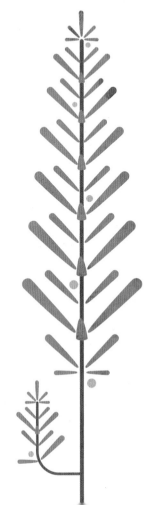

Corn Chowder

and FRIED ZUCCHINI SANDWICH

Aren't you excited to unpack the sweaters, light the fire pits, and cook up food that warms from the inside out when the weather starts to chill? This fall soup makes the most of the last gasp of corn and zucchini season. Though late-summer corn can be a little starchy for eating straight off the cob, those starches and sugars make a delicious bowl of rich, creamy chowder. And on the side, you're going to love the crispy fried zucchini sandwich slathered with hummus.

¼ cup [35 g] all-purpose flour

1 egg, beaten

¾ cup [45 g] panko bread crumbs

One 6-in [15-cm] zucchini, cut lengthwise into ¼-in [6-mm] slices

Kosher salt and freshly ground black pepper

2 Tbsp olive oil, plus more as needed

1 onion, chopped

½ stalk celery, chopped

1 garlic clove, minced

¼ tsp dried oregano

2 cups [280 g] fresh or frozen corn

2 cups [480 ml] vegetable broth

½ cup [120 ml] milk

Pinch of cayenne pepper

2 pita breads

Hummus, sliced tomato, lettuce, and sliced red onion for serving

1 sprig fresh basil, leaves thinly sliced

---

1. Put the flour, egg, and panko in three separate shallow bowls. Season the zucchini slices with salt and black pepper, dredge them in the flour, and shake off the excess. Dip in the egg, then coat well with the panko. Set aside on a cutting board or sheet pan.

2. Heat a 12-in [30.5-cm] skillet over medium-high heat, and add the olive oil. When the oil shimmers, add the zucchini slices in batches and cook until browned on both sides, about 4 minutes, adding more oil if necessary. Transfer the zucchini to a paper towel–lined plate and keep warm.

continued

3. Add the onion, celery, garlic, and oregano to the hot pan, along with a little more oil if necessary. Sauté until the onion begins to soften, about 3 minutes. Add the corn, vegetable broth, milk, cayenne, ¼ tsp salt, and a few grinds of black pepper and bring to a simmer. Turn the heat to low so that the soup just bubbles. Cook until the vegetables are tender and flavors have blended, about 10 minutes. Taste and season with more salt and black pepper, if it needs it.

4. Halve the pitas and split them open to make pockets. Sandwich the fried zucchini and some hummus into the pita halves, along with tomato, lettuce, and onion.

5. Ladle the soup into heated bowls and sprinkle with basil. Serve immediately with the pita sandwich.

It's that easy: *To make this soup even cornier, add the stripped cobs to the soup while it cooks. (Discard before serving.) It's amazing how much corn essence ekes out of the cobs after just a few minutes of cooking. Plus, you can pat yourself on the back for extracting extra flavor from something that most cooks would have just tossed in the compost heap.*

Extra hungry? *Fry up an extra zucchini for additional sandwiches.*

In the glass: *A well-chilled Riesling or Chardonnay is a great accompaniment to this simple supper.*

START TO FINISH
40 minutes
· · ·
HANDS-ON TIME
25 minutes
· · ·
Serves 2

Minestrone

with HERBED DUMPLINGS

Maybe the most famous of the Italian soups, minestrone is like eating a garden in a bowl. Simple vegetables, beans, and sometimes pasta are combined with broth to create a hearty and delicious meal that has fed the people of Italy for centuries. Like little boats floating off the coast of Naples, the herbed dumplings dotting this soup take this dish into deliciously uncharted waters.

2 Tbsp olive oil

1 onion, diced

1 stalk celery, diced

1 carrot, sliced

One 6-in [15-cm] zucchini, halved lengthwise and sliced

1/2 tsp dried basil

Kosher salt and freshly ground black pepper

One 15-oz [425-g] can cannellini beans, drained

One 14 1/2-oz [411-g] can diced tomatoes with juice

2 cups [480 ml] vegetable broth, plus more as needed

1/2 cup [70 g] all-purpose flour

1/2 tsp baking powder

1/4 cup [60 ml] milk

1 Tbsp unsalted butter, melted

2 Tbsp minced fresh flat-leaf parsley

2 Tbsp chopped fresh basil

1/2 lemon, cut into wedges

1/4 cup [8 g] grated Parmesan cheese

1. Heat a 12-in [30.5-cm] skillet or 3-qt [2.8-L] saucepan over medium-high heat, and add the olive oil. When the oil shimmers, add the onion, celery, carrot, zucchini, dried basil, 1/2 tsp salt, and a few grinds of pepper. Sauté until the vegetables begin to soften, about 3 minutes. Add the beans, tomatoes, and vegetable broth and bring to a simmer. Turn the heat to low, cover, and simmer for about 5 minutes to get the cooking started.

2. Meanwhile, in a medium bowl, stir together the flour, baking powder, milk, butter, 1/4 tsp salt, and 1 Tbsp of the parsley just until combined.

3. Drop the mixture by the tablespoonful into the simmering stew, about eight dollops, cover, and simmer until the vegetables and dumplings are tender, about 15 minutes. Don't peek; the steam will

continued

be released and your dumplings may not be as puffy and light as they could be. Test for doneness by running a toothpick into a dumpling; it should come out with dry crumbs adhering to it. If the dumpling is still wet and gooey, cover, cook 3 minutes longer, and check again.

4. Ladle the soup and dumplings into heated bowls and sprinkle with the fresh basil and remaining 1 Tbsp parsley. Serve with the lemon wedges and Parmesan on the side.

It's that easy: *Canned beans and tomatoes are relatively cheap, so you can buy the best for only a few pennies more. Find a brand that suits you and then stick with it, whether a store brand, national label, or organic.*

Extra hungry? *Double the dumpling mixture and give it another few minutes of cooking time. You may find less broth in the soup because the dumplings will absorb some of it, so add a little more broth as needed.*

In the glass: *There's a lot of flavor going on in this soup. Try a soft, easygoing Pinot Grigio.*

African Peanut Stew

with BRAAIBROODJIE

This African-inspired stew, one of my favorites in the soupy spectrum, is a carnival of flavors, with rich peanut, ginger, curry, lime, and sweet potato paired with the South African version of a panini. The word *braaibroodjie* (bry-BROOD-she; say it three times fast) sounds unusual but this dish will charm you with its meltingly salty-sharp cheese, tart chutney, onion, and tomato between raisin-laced brown bread. Yum.

4 slices raisin bread or other home-style bread	2 tsp curry powder
2 Tbsp mayonnaise	One 14½-oz [411-g] can diced tomatoes with juice
½ cup [40 g] grated sharp Cheddar cheese	2 cups [480 ml] vegetable broth
1 small tomato, sliced	⅓ cup [70 g] chunky peanut butter
1 onion; half thinly sliced, half diced	1 small sweet potato, cut into ½-in [12-mm] dice
2 Tbsp Major Grey's chutney	½ cup [70 g] frozen green beans, thawed
2 Tbsp vegetable oil	Kosher salt and freshly ground black pepper
1 garlic clove, chopped	1 lime, cut into wedges
1 serrano chile, seeded and minced	2 Tbsp chopped peanuts
One 2-in [5-cm] knob fresh ginger, peeled and chopped	2 Tbsp chopped fresh cilantro

1. Spread one side of each slice of bread with the mayonnaise. Lay two of the slices mayo-side down, sprinkle with the cheese, and lay the sliced tomato and onion on top. Spread the uncovered side of the remaining bread slices with the chutney. Cover the onion with the bread slices, chutney-side down/mayo-side up.

2. Heat a 12-in [30.5-cm] skillet over medium-high heat, and cook the sandwiches, undisturbed, for 2 minutes, then check to see if they're browned. Flip them with a wide spatula and brown the other side until the insides are heated through and the outside is browned, about 2 minutes longer. Transfer the sandwiches to a plate and keep warm.

3. Add the vegetable oil to the hot pan. When the oil shimmers, add the diced onion, garlic, chile, ginger, and curry powder and cook until fragrant, about 1 minute. Add the diced tomatoes, vegetable broth, peanut butter, sweet potato, green beans, $^{1}/_{4}$ tsp salt, and a few grinds of pepper and bring to a simmer. Turn the heat to low and simmer until the sweet potato is tender, about 15 minutes. Add a squeeze of lime. Taste and season with more salt and pepper, if it needs it.

4. Ladle the stew into heated bowls and top with the peanuts, cilantro, and a lime wedge. Cut the warm sandwiches in half and serve on the side.

It's that easy: *It can be a chore to peel around ginger's knobs and crevices, but not when you use the tip of a spoon to scrape away the pesky skin. Try it. You won't believe how easy and fast peeling ginger can be.*

Extra hungry? *You can always make another sandwich or toss a little leftover cooked rice into the stew.*

In the glass: *Something from one of your local breweries would be a fine choice. My pick would be Thirsty Dog Old Druid Bloodhound Saison French ale if you can find it.*

Moroccan Chickpea Stew

with HARISSA and NAAN

This North African spicy stew not only tastes good but is good for you too. I crave it in January after all the culinary debauchery of the holidays, as this kind of brew puts my diet back on track. The harissa really adds a spicy character, so don't skimp on it. Sure, it's hot, but it's also flavorful, rich, and smoky. You can adjust the harissa to suit your tastes but I usually make this a little hotter than is comfortable in order to shock my system back into a healthy rhythm, much like a defibrillator shocks the heart.

1 Tbsp unsalted butter	One 14½-oz [411-g] can diced tomatoes with juice
1 small onion, sliced	One 15-oz [425-g] can chickpeas, drained
1 carrot, sliced	2 cups [480 ml] vegetable broth, plus more as needed
1 garlic clove, chopped	¼ cup [45 g] brown lentils, sorted and rinsed
¼ tsp ground cinnamon	1 to 2 tsp harissa
¼ tsp ground cumin	½ lemon
Pinch of ground ginger	2 Tbsp chopped fresh cilantro
Pinch of ground turmeric	Naan or other flatbread for serving
Kosher salt and freshly ground black pepper	

1. Heat a 3-qt [2.8-L] saucepan over medium-high heat, and melt the butter. When the butter sizzles, add the onion, carrot, garlic, cinnamon, cumin, ginger, turmeric, ¼ tsp salt, and a few grinds of pepper. Sauté until the spices are fragrant and the onion softens, about 2 minutes. Add the tomatoes, chickpeas, vegetable broth, and lentils and bring to a simmer. Turn the heat to low and simmer until the lentils are tender, about 20 minutes. If you'd like a thinner soup, add a little more broth until it seems right.

2. Stir in the harissa, ½ tsp at a time, depending on how spicy you like your soup. Taste and season with more salt and pepper, if it needs it.

3. Ladle the stew into heated bowls, add a squeeze of lemon, and sprinkle with the cilantro. Serve with naan on the side.

It's that easy: *Harissa is a spicy North African chile paste that has been referred to as Moroccan ketchup. It's based on roasted red peppers, garlic, hot chiles, cumin, coriander, lemon, and oil and can be found in ethnic markets, online, and at some grocery stores. Use it to kick up the flavor in rice dishes and couscous, as a rub on meats, or stirred into roasted vegetables.*

Extra hungry? *Serve some hummus on the side as a dip for the naan.*

In the glass: *I like this stew on the spicy side, so look for something like mint tea to go along with it. If you're looking for an adult beverage, try your favorite beer.*

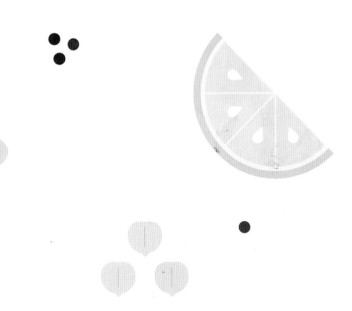

Kidney Bean Masala

Rajma is a classic Indian kidney bean curry with tomato, onion, and lots of spices. The deep, dark kidney beans infused with garlic, ginger, cinnamon, coriander, and turmeric is a perfect example of how a really simple dish can deliver remarkably complex flavors. This is a celebratory meal, but don't wait for a special occasion to make it.

2 Tbsp vegetable oil

1 onion, diced

One 2-in [5-cm] knob fresh ginger, peeled and minced

2 garlic cloves, minced

1 cinnamon stick

1 bay leaf

2 tsp coriander seeds, ground in a mortar and pestle, or ½ tsp ground coriander

½ tsp ground turmeric

¼ tsp cayenne pepper, plus more as needed

Pinch of ground cloves

Kosher salt and freshly ground black pepper

One 14½-oz [411-g] can diced tomatoes with juice

One 15-oz [425-g] can dark red kidney beans, drained and rinsed

1 cup [240 ml] vegetable broth

Cooked rice for serving

1 Tbsp minced fresh cilantro

1. Heat a 12-in [30.5-cm] skillet or 3-qt [2.8-L] saucepan over medium-high heat, and add the vegetable oil. When the oil shimmers, add the onion and ginger. Sauté until the onion begins to soften, about 2 minutes. Add the garlic, cinnamon, bay leaf, coriander, turmeric, cayenne, cloves, ½ tsp salt, and a few grinds of black pepper. Sauté, stirring, until the spices are fragrant, about 2 minutes. Add the tomatoes, beans, and vegetable broth and bring to a simmer. Turn the heat to low, cover, and simmer until the flavors blend, about 10 minutes.

2. Carefully remove the bay leaf and cinnamon stick. Taste and season with more salt, black pepper, and cayenne, if it needs it.

3. Ladle the masala into heated bowls over rice. Sprinkle with the cilantro before serving.

continued

WARMING SOUPS & STEWS

It's that easy: *A mortar and pestle is a fine tool to have, as it allows you to freshly grind spices (which are way more delicious and aromatic when freshly ground). Mine is made of marble but ceramic or lava rock is good as well. If you don't want to invest in one, buy an inexpensive coffee mill and use it exclusively to grind spices. You'll be astonished by the difference in taste.*

Extra hungry? *Serve with some naan, a delicious flatbread from Asia.*

In the glass: *A light and lemony shandy would be a fine accompaniment.*

START TO FINISH
45 minutes
. . .
HANDS-ON TIME
25 minutes
. . .
Serves 2

Two-Bean Chili

with CHIPOTLE *and* CORN BREAD DUMPLINGS

Pinto beans and deep, dark kidney beans team up to make this rib-sticking meal a weekday favorite. Adding a can of Ro-Tel tomatoes makes perfect sense, since some onions and chiles are already added. But the star of this dish is the chipotle chile, which chimes in with its smoky heat (careful you don't hurt yourself), while little cornmeal dumplings eliminate the need for any other sides.

2 Tbsp olive oil

1 onion, diced

1 small poblano chile, seeded, deribbed, and diced

1 garlic clove, minced

1 Tbsp chili powder

½ tsp dried oregano

½ canned chipotle chile, minced

One 15-oz [425-g] can pinto beans, drained and rinsed

One 15-oz [425-g] can dark red kidney beans, drained and rinsed

One 10-oz [283-g] can Ro-Tel tomatoes with chiles, with juice

2 cups [480 ml] vegetable broth

1 tsp cider vinegar

Kosher salt

⅔ cup [90 g] all-purpose flour

⅓ cup [40 g] yellow cornmeal

1 Tbsp sugar

1 tsp baking powder

2 Tbsp unsalted butter, at room temperature

½ cup [120 ml] milk

Sour cream, shredded Monterey Jack cheese, and chopped fresh cilantro for garnish (optional)

1. Heat a 3-qt [2.8-L] pot over medium heat, and add the olive oil. When the oil shimmers, add the onion. Sauté until the onion begins to soften, about 2 minutes. Add the poblano, garlic, chili powder, oregano, and chipotle and sauté, stirring, until the poblano is tender, about 5 minutes. Add the pinto beans, kidney beans, tomatoes, vegetable broth, vinegar, and ½ tsp salt and bring to a simmer. Turn the heat to medium-low, cover, and simmer until the flavors blend, about 10 minutes.

continued

WARMING SOUPS & STEWS

39

2. Meanwhile, in a medium bowl, combine the flour, cornmeal, sugar, baking powder, and $1/4$ tsp salt. Add the butter and blend it into the flour, using a snapping motion with your thumbs and fingers. It's okay if it's still a little lumpy. Pour in the milk and mix with a fork until just moistened. Be careful not to overmix or your dumplings will be tough.

3. Drop the mixture by the heaping tablespoonful around the circumference of the pot, leaving enough space between the dumplings so they can expand. Cover and simmer until the dumplings are cooked through, about 15 minutes. Don't peek; the steam will be released and your dumplings may not be as puffy and light as they could be. Test for doneness by running a toothpick into a dumpling; it should come out with dry crumbs adhering to it. If the dumpling is still wet and gooey, cover, cook 3 minutes longer, and check again.

4. Ladle the chili and dumplings into heated bowls. Garnish with sour cream and sprinkle with cheese and cilantro, if desired, before serving.

It's that easy: Chipotle chiles are hot, hot, hot, so if you're sensitive to heat, just add a tiny bit to get started and then add more if you want it spicier. Remember, you can't take it out once it's in there!

Extra hungry? Add some diced avocado to beef up the chili if need be.

In the glass: A beer. A really nice cold one.

CHAPTER

2

Eggs & Cheese, Please

Ricotta Frittata

with SPINACH, CORN, *and* SUN-DRIED TOMATO

Ricotta adds cheesy heft to this weeknight staple that's loaded with spinach, mushrooms, and corn and studded with sun-dried tomatoes and feta cheese. It's a farmers' market in a skillet.

---

5 eggs

⅓ cup [80 g] ricotta cheese

¼ cup [8 g] grated Parmesan cheese

¼ cup [60 ml] milk

Pinch of freshly grated nutmeg

Kosher salt and freshly ground black pepper

2 Tbsp olive oil

1 small onion, sliced

1 garlic clove, minced

4 oz [115 g] mushrooms, chopped

12 oz [340 g] baby spinach

1 cup [140 g] frozen corn

⅓ cup [60 g] chopped oil-packed sun-dried tomatoes, drained

¼ cup [30 g] crumbled feta cheese

---

1. Place an oven rack in the second highest position and preheat the broiler.

2. In a medium bowl, whisk together the eggs, ricotta, Parmesan, milk, nutmeg, ½ tsp salt, and a few grinds of pepper. Set aside.

3. Heat a 12-in [30.5-cm] oven-safe skillet over medium-high heat, and add the olive oil. When the oil shimmers, add the onion and sauté until it begins to soften, about 2 minutes. Add the garlic and mushrooms and cook until the mushrooms begin to soften, about 3 minutes. Add the spinach by the handful, letting it wilt before adding more.

Season with salt and pepper and cook until the spinach is tender, about 2 minutes. Stir in the corn and sun-dried tomatoes and cook until the liquid in the bottom of the pan evaporates, about 2 minutes.

4. Spread the vegetables evenly in the skillet, sprinkle the feta over the top, and pour the egg mixture evenly over all. Turn the heat to low, cover, and cook for 2 minutes. Uncover and transfer the pan to the oven. Broil the frittata until the top is lightly browned and puffed and the center is firm, about 4 minutes. To test, press the center of the frittata lightly with your finger (careful, it's hot). If it feels firm, it's done.

5. Remove the frittata from the oven and let sit for 5 minutes. It will be puffy when it comes out of the oven but will deflate and become firmer as it cools. Cut into wedges and serve hot or at room temperature.

It's that easy: Once you get the hang of it, frittatas are a terrific way of cleaning out the crisper and cheese drawers in your fridge. Just sauté leftover greens such as arugula, escarole, spinach, chard, and kale; grate up the bits and pieces of leftover cheeses; toss with some eggs; and call it dinner.

Extra hungry? Add a refreshing salad of Boston lettuce, diced oranges, olives, and thinly sliced fennel with a splash of white wine vinegar and a glug of olive oil.

In the glass: A Sauvignon Blanc from Frog's Leap would be delicious with this simple meal, as would a glass of New Zealand Pinot Noir, if you're in the mood for a red. Look for Delta Vineyard Pinot Noir or Crossroads Destination Series Pinot Noir for great, food-friendly bottles.

Persian Zucchini Frittata

Turmeric, grated zucchini, and caramelized red onion add Middle Eastern flair to this easy-to-make weeknight staple. By the way, it's worth buying a pomegranate just for this dish. The little ruby seeds add fun in the way of color, pop, and bright acidity to this simple yet decadent weeknight meal.

2 Tbsp olive oil

1 small red onion, thinly sliced

One 2-in [5-cm] knob fresh ginger, peeled and minced

1 garlic clove, minced

½ tsp ground turmeric

Two 6-in [15-cm] zucchini, grated

Kosher salt and freshly ground black pepper

¾ cup [150 g] cooked rice

4 eggs, beaten with 2 Tbsp water and a pinch of kosher salt

2 Tbsp minced fresh flat-leaf parsley

Pomegranate seeds for garnish (optional)

1. Place an oven rack in the second highest position and preheat the broiler.

2. Heat a 12-in [30.5-cm] oven-safe skillet over medium-high heat, and add the olive oil. When the oil shimmers, add the onion and sauté until it begins to soften, about 2 minutes. Turn the heat to medium and cook, stirring every now and then, until the onion browns, about 6 minutes. Stir in the ginger, garlic, and turmeric and cook until the garlic is fragrant, about 2 minutes.

3. Turn the heat to medium-high and add the zucchini, ½ tsp salt, and a few grinds of pepper. Cook until the zucchini is tender, about 3 minutes. Stir in the rice until well combined.

4. Spread the vegetable-rice mixture evenly in the skillet and pour the eggs evenly over them. Turn the heat to low, cover, and cook for 2 minutes. Uncover and transfer the pan to the oven. Broil the frittata until the top is lightly browned and puffed and the center is firm, about 3 minutes. To test, press the center of the frittata lightly with your finger (careful, it's hot). If it feels firm, it's done.

5. Remove the frittata from the oven and let sit for 5 minutes. It will be puffy when it comes out of the oven but will deflate and become firmer as it cools. Garnish with the parsley and pomegranate seeds, if desired. Cut into wedges and serve hot or at room temperature.

It's that easy: Rice bulks up this frittata and makes it more of a stand-alone meal. Use leftover takeout rice or precooked frozen rice. You can use white rice, but why not go for more nutrition and use brown rice instead?

Extra hungry? Just add another egg or two if you're feeling more hungry than usual.

In the glass: Acrobat Pinot Gris from King Estate is sure to make you happy.

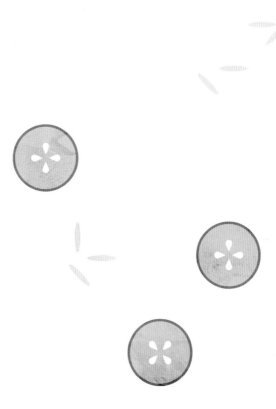

Potato Frittata à l'Indienne

This frittata emigrates from Italy to India with a side trip to France by including vadouvan, a French-inspired curry powder. I've kept it simple with only potatoes in the filling, but the taste is anything but. Don't let the vadouvan scare you away from this recipe. Any curry powder will do, though the vadouvan is pretty special. Look for it online and order a jar. You won't be sorry.

6 eggs	Kosher salt and freshly ground black pepper
2 Tbsp minced fresh cilantro	2 garlic cloves, minced
2 Tbsp olive oil	1 serrano chile, seeded and minced
1 onion, diced	1½ tsp vadouvan or curry powder
4 new potatoes, cut into ½-in [12-mm] dice	1 cup [140 g] grape tomatoes, halved

1. Place an oven rack in the second highest position and preheat the broiler.

2. In a medium bowl, whisk together the eggs and 1 Tbsp of the cilantro. Set aside.

3. Heat a 12-in [30.5-cm] oven-safe skillet over medium-high heat, and add the olive oil. When the oil shimmers, add the onion, potatoes, ½ tsp salt, and a few grinds of pepper and stir to coat the onion and potatoes in the oil. Cook, undisturbed, for 3 minutes, then turn the vegetables with a spatula and cook for 3 minutes longer. Turn them again and cook until they are browned and tender, about 3 minutes longer. Add the garlic, serrano, and vadouvan and cook, stirring, until the garlic is fragrant and the flavors have blended, about 1 minute.

4. Spread the vegetables evenly in the skillet and pour the eggs evenly over them. Turn the heat to low, cover, and cook for 2 minutes. Uncover and transfer the pan to the oven. Broil the frittata until the top is lightly browned and puffed and the center is firm, about 2 minutes. To test, press the center of the frittata lightly with your finger (careful, it's hot). If it feels firm, it's done.

5. Remove the frittata from the oven and let sit for 5 minutes. It will be puffy when it comes out of the oven but will deflate and become firmer as it cools. Garnish with the tomatoes and remaining 1 Tbsp cilantro. Cut into wedges and serve hot or at room temperature.

It's that easy: Don't skimp on the vadouvan or curry powder here. The better and fresher the spices, the better the flavor of your dish. So if you have a jar of curry powder that's been sitting in your pantry for years, it's probably time to toss it. Start out fresh and buy a new jar, preferably from an online source that has good turnover like Penzeys or Spice House.

Extra hungry? Toss sliced cucumbers with a thinly sliced red onion, a squeeze of lemon, a spoonful of yogurt, and a glug of olive oil for a refreshingly cool salad.

In the glass: Egg dishes love sparkling wine, and Freixenet Cava will love this frittata right back.

Tortilla Española

A traditional tapas favorite, this egg and potato dish can be found in almost every tapas bar in Spain. Designed to curb hunger pangs with cocktails before that ten o'clock Spanish dinner, it makes a fine American dinner at six o'clock as well.

4 eggs

2 Tbsp chopped fresh flat-leaf parsley

Kosher salt and freshly ground black pepper

¼ cup [60 ml] olive oil

2 russet potatoes, peeled and cut into ½-in [12-mm] dice

1 small onion, diced

1 garlic clove, minced

1 tomato, seeded and diced

1. Place an oven rack in the second highest position and preheat the broiler.

2. In a large bowl, whisk together the eggs, parsley, a pinch of salt, and a few grinds of pepper. Set aside.

3. Heat a 12-in [30.5-cm] oven-safe skillet over medium-high heat, and add the olive oil. When the oil shimmers, add the potatoes, ¼ tsp salt, and a few grinds of pepper and stir to coat the potatoes in the oil. Cook the potatoes, tossing them every now and then, until crispy on the outside and tender on the inside, about 10 minutes.

4. Add the onion to the pan and sauté until translucent, about 3 minutes. Turn the heat to medium, add the garlic, and sauté until fragrant, about 2 minutes. Stir in the tomato, ¼ tsp salt, and a few grinds of pepper and cook until the tomato has broken down,

about 2 minutes. The mixture will become liquidy from the tomatoes, so turn the heat to low if it starts to spatter.

5. Spread the vegetables evenly in the skillet and pour the eggs evenly over them. Turn the heat to low, cover, and cook for 5 minutes. Uncover and transfer the pan to the oven. Broil the tortilla until it is set, about 3 minutes. To test, press the center of the tortilla lightly with your finger (careful, it's hot). If it feels firm, it's done.

6. Remove the tortilla from the oven and let sit for 5 minutes. It will be puffy when it comes out of the oven but will deflate and become firmer as it cools. Cut into wedges and serve warm or at room temperature.

continued

EGGS & CHEESE, PLEASE

It's that easy: To quickly dice the potatoes, halve one lengthwise. Lay one half flat-side down and cut it into ½-in [12-mm] slices. Lay a stack of slices flat on their side and cut into ½-in [12-mm] sticks, then cut from the short side into cubes.

Extra hungry? A green salad would be refreshingly welcome with this sturdy meal. How about torn romaine leaves tossed with a squeeze of lemon, a glug of olive oil, and a sprinkle of Parmesan?

In the glass: Gotta go Spanish here with a Marqués de Cáceres Rioja. Olé!

Italian Omelet

with MUSHROOM, FONTINA, and BASIL

When I'm tired and don't know what to eat, an omelet is the perfect ending to an imperfect day. I clean out the fridge of dibs and dabs of cheese, the last few grape tomatoes, or bunches of greens or other veggies, setting my small world in order. Then I enjoy the process of cooking the omelet and turning it out onto my plate in perfect form—or not. Even if it breaks and the filling spills out, at least the fridge has been somewhat organized and I have a tasty, hot meal.

6 eggs	2 Tbsp olive oil
Kosher salt and freshly ground black pepper	1 onion, diced
½ cup [40 g] grated fontina cheese	4 baby bella or cremini mushrooms, thinly sliced
2 Tbsp grated Parmesan cheese	1 garlic clove, minced
12 halved grape tomatoes	4 oz [115 g] baby spinach
Leaves from 3 sprigs fresh basil, sliced	2 Tbsp unsalted butter
1 tsp red wine vinegar	

1. In a medium bowl, whisk together the eggs, 2 Tbsp water, ¼ tsp salt, and a few grinds of pepper. Set aside.

2. In a small bowl, combine the fontina and Parmesan. Set aside.

3. In a medium bowl, toss together the tomatoes, basil, vinegar, 1 Tbsp of the olive oil, a pinch of salt, and a few grinds of pepper. Set aside.

4. Heat a 10-in [25-cm] nonstick skillet over medium-high heat, and add the remaining 1 Tbsp olive oil. When the oil shimmers, add the onion and sauté until translucent, about 1 minute. Add the mushrooms and cook until tender, about 3 minutes. Add the garlic, spinach, a pinch of salt, and a few grinds of pepper and cook until the spinach wilts, about 1 minute. Transfer the vegetables to a plate and keep warm. Do not wipe the pan.

continued

5. Melt 1 Tbsp of the butter in the hot pan. When the butter sizzles, add half of the eggs and swirl so that they evenly cover the bottom of the pan. Using a spatula, lift up the sides of the cooked egg, allowing the uncooked egg to flow to the bottom of the pan. Cook until the egg sets, about 1 minute. Slide the pan off the heat and place half of the cooked vegetable mixture and half of the cheese mixture down the center of the omelet. Use the spatula to gently fold one-third of the omelet over the filling, followed by the other side up and over, like a business letter. Return the pan to the heat and cook to warm the middle, about 30 seconds. Slide the omelet out of the pan, flipping it upside down onto a heated plate (this may take a bit of practice, but it will still be delicious even if it isn't perfect). Keep warm. Make a second omelet with the remaining 1 Tbsp butter and the remaining egg, vegetable, and cheese mixtures.

6. Top the omelets with the tomato mixture. Serve hot.

It's that easy: Cheese makes a dinner to dream about. You can stuff just about any kind of soft to medium cheese inside as long as it melts nicely. My faves are fontina, Brie, Monterey Jack, colby, Swiss . . . you get the picture!

Extra hungry? Toast up big slices of country-style bread drizzled with olive oil and make an omelet sandwich.

In the glass: Something light and fruity like a Pinot Grigio from Ménage à Trois or a sparkling Prosecco from Mionetto are sure to pair well.

Eggs Florentine

Eggs Florentine is the kind of retro, swanky dish I imagine my grandparents ate for brunch at the Breakers Hotel in the '80s. Traditionally, eggs Florentine includes sautéed spinach with a poached egg and hollandaise sauce, which can be delicious though a bit fussy. Since most of us don't feel like whisking melted butter slowly into hot egg yolks (careful or they'll scramble!) to make hollandaise for a weeknight meal, I came up with an easier way. I just cream the spinach and then poach the eggs on top, all in one pan. Though not completely faithful to the old-school version, I'm sure Grandma would approve.

2 Tbsp olive oil, plus more for drizzling	1/3 cup [80 ml] heavy cream
1 onion, diced	Pinch of freshly grated nutmeg
6 oz [170 g] baby spinach or a mix of spinach and arugula	1 tsp fresh lemon juice
	4 eggs
Kosher salt and freshly ground black pepper	4 English muffins, split

1. Heat a 12-in [30.5-cm] skillet over medium-high heat, and add the olive oil. When the oil shimmers, add the onion and sauté until it begins to soften, about 3 minutes. Add the spinach by the handful, letting it wilt before adding more. Add 1/4 tsp salt and a few grinds of pepper and cook until the liquid in the bottom of the pan evaporates, about 1 minute. Stir in the cream, nutmeg, and lemon juice.

2. Turn the heat to medium-low and simmer until the cream thickens slightly, about 1 minute. Crack the eggs and slide them gently out of their shells and on top of the spinach. Don't break the yolks! Season the eggs with salt and pepper, cover, and cook until the whites are set but the yolks are still runny, about 3 minutes. For firmer yolks, turn off the heat and let the eggs sit in the skillet, covered, for 1 minute longer. The residual heat in the pan will continue to cook the eggs.

3. Meanwhile, drizzle the cut sides of the English muffins with a little olive oil and toast in a toaster.

4. Place two muffin halves on each of two heated plates. With a large spoon or spatula, carefully scoop out some of the greens and one egg and lay on one muffin half. Scoop the remaining eggs and spinach onto the other muffin halves in the same way. Top with the remaining halves of the muffins and eat them with your hands (like my husband), or leave them open-faced and eat with a knife and fork (like me).

It's that easy: Brunchy dishes like eggs Florentine slide easily onto our veggie-only dinner menus. And now that eggs are good for us again (whew!), I make it a point to buy the best organic, free-range eggs I can find. The best eggs I've sourced are from my local farmers' market, where I've come to know and trust the purveyors.

Extra hungry? You can always add another egg.

In the glass: White and fizzy rules the day. Look for a white sparkler like a Crémant d'Alsace brut rosé from Wolfberger.

Bibimbap

with FRIED EGG

Bibimbap (BEE-bim-bop) is a delicious Korean dish of rice, sautéed vegetables, fried egg, spicy chile sauce, and kimchi. Gochujang is a chile sauce; and though it may take a trip to your Asian market to find it, you'll be so glad to have this flavorful condiment in your fridge the next time you want to make a tasty barbecue sauce or glaze. Traditionally, the vegetables in bibimbap are cooked separately and arranged beautifully on top of the rice, but I think you'll appreciate the time-saving measure of just cooking all the veggies at once. After all, you're going to mix it all up before you take the first bite, right?

Sauce

2 Tbsp gochujang

2 Tbsp mirin or white wine

2 tsp sugar

2 tsp sesame seeds

1 tsp sesame oil

3 Tbsp vegetable oil

2 garlic cloves, minced

One 2-in [5-cm] knob fresh ginger, peeled and minced

1 head broccoli, florets chopped and stalk sliced as thinly as possible

½ cup [30 g] coarsely chopped snow peas

1 carrot, julienned

One 6-in [15-cm] zucchini, halved lengthwise and thinly sliced

8 shiitake mushrooms, stemmed and thinly sliced

2 Tbsp soy sauce, plus more as needed

1 Tbsp mirin

1 Tbsp sesame oil, plus more as needed

1½ cups [290 g] cooked rice

2 eggs

2 green onions, white and green parts, thinly sliced

½ cup [100 g] kimchi

continued

1. To make the sauce: In a small bowl, combine the gochujang, mirin, sugar, sesame seeds, and sesame oil. Set aside.

2. Heat a 12-in [30.5-cm] skillet over medium-high heat, and add 2 Tbsp of the vegetable oil. When the oil shimmers, add the garlic, ginger, and broccoli and sauté until fragrant, about 1 minute. Add the snow peas, carrot, zucchini, and mushrooms and sauté until the vegetables begin to get tender, about 3 minutes.

3. Meanwhile, in a small bowl, combine the soy sauce, mirin, and sesame oil. Pour the mixture over the vegetables and stir and cook until the vegetables are crisp-tender, about 1 minute. Taste and add more soy sauce or sesame oil, if it needs it.

4. Spoon the cooked rice into two heated bowls, top with the cooked vegetables, and keep warm.

5. Add the remaining 1 Tbsp vegetable oil to the hot pan. When the oil shimmers, gently break the eggs into the pan and cook until the whites are set but the yolks are still runny, about 2 minutes.

6. With a thin spatula, carefully place the eggs on top of the vegetables. (Don't worry if your egg yolk breaks since you'll be mixing it all together anyway.) Garnish each with the green onions, half the kimchi, and 1 to 2 tsp of the sauce. Mix it all together with your fork and eat it up before it gets cold.

It's that easy: Sometimes when you cook everything for a meal in one pan, the bottom of the pan can get a little torched. After frying the egg for this dish, the bottom of the pan will need a little extra cleaning. If you scrub the pan with Bar Keepers Friend (either powder or liquid), it will sparkle in no time flat. Buy a can; you won't be sorry.

Extra hungry? Fry another egg or two.

In the glass: Riesling is the one wine that can stand up to the spice and heat going on in this dish. Look for Kendall-Jackson Vintner's Reserve Riesling. It's a great buy.

Shakshuka

with NEW POTATOES

Shakshuka (shak-SHOE-kuh) is a Tunisian dish of tomatoes, chiles, spices, and eggs. It's remarkably fast and easy to make and astonishingly delicious, which makes it a perfect weeknight meal. In this version, I've included potatoes in order to make it more dinner-ish and added feta cheese just for fun.

2 Tbsp olive oil	¼ tsp ground cumin
2 or 3 new potatoes, cut into ¼-in [6-mm] dice	One 14½-oz [411-g] can diced tomatoes with juice
Kosher salt and freshly ground black pepper	2 tsp honey
1 onion, diced	1 tsp red wine vinegar
1 serrano chile, seeded and minced	3 eggs
2 garlic cloves, minced	⅓ cup [40 g] crumbled feta cheese
1 Tbsp harissa	2 Tbsp minced fresh flat-leaf parsley
1 tsp paprika	Toasted country-style bread slices for serving

1. Heat a 12-in [30.5-cm] skillet or 3-qt [2.8-L] saucepan over medium-high heat, and add the olive oil. When the oil shimmers, add the potatoes, ½ tsp salt, and a few grinds of pepper and stir to coat the potatoes in the oil. Cook, undisturbed, for 3 minutes, then turn the potatoes with a spatula and cook until they are browned and tender, 3 minutes longer. Add the onion, serrano, and garlic and cook until the onion is tender, about 3 minutes. Add the harissa, paprika, and cumin and cook, stirring, until fragrant, about 1 minute. Add the tomatoes, honey, and vinegar and bring to a boil. Turn the heat to low and simmer until the sauce thickens, about 3 minutes.

2. With a large spoon, make three shallow indentations in the sauce. Crack the eggs and slide them gently out of their shells and into the indentations. Don't break the yolks! Season the eggs with salt and pepper, cover, and cook until the whites are set but the yolks are still runny, about 3 minutes. For firmer yolks, turn off the heat and let the eggs sit in the skillet, covered, for 2 minutes longer. The residual heat in the pan will continue to cook the eggs. Sprinkle the feta and parsley over the top.

continued

3. Divide the shakshuka among heated bowls and serve hot with bread on the side.

It's that easy: Shakshuka also makes a fine brunch dish for a crowd. Just use a bigger pan and triple the recipe.

Extra hungry? Add another egg or two.

In the glass: Shakshuka is on the spicy side, so a Gewürztraminer or Riesling is in order here. Look for a bottle from Chateau Ste. Michelle.

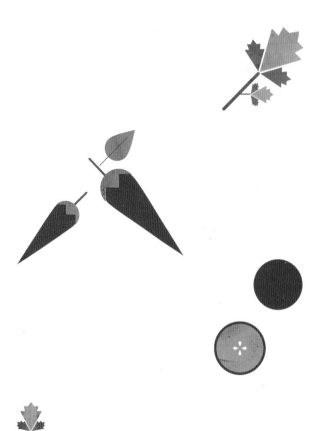

Huevos Rancheros

with BLACK BEANS

Huevos rancheros (WEH-vohs ran-CHAIR-ohs) is translated as "ranch-style eggs," and if I worked on a ranch, I'd want to eat a meal like this every day. There are countless variations on the theme of tomatoes, eggs, tortillas, and cheese, but I'm betting you'll be partial to this one-pan wonder. In this version, I've also included black beans for extra heft.

2 Tbsp vegetable oil

1 onion, diced

2 garlic cloves, minced

6 plum tomatoes, quartered, seeded, and chopped

1 tsp chili powder

Kosher salt and freshly ground black pepper

One 15-oz [425-g] can black beans, drained and rinsed

⅓ cup [80 ml] vegetable broth

1 tsp honey

2 Tbsp chopped fresh cilantro, plus more for garnish

4 eggs

Four 6-in [15-cm] corn tortillas

½ cup [60 g] crumbled queso fresco

1. Preheat the oven to 450°F [230°C].

2. Heat a 12-in [30.5-cm] skillet over medium-high heat, and add the vegetable oil. When the oil shimmers, add the onion and garlic and sauté until the onion begins to soften, about 1 minute. Add the tomatoes, chili powder, ½ tsp salt, and a few grinds of pepper. Sauté until the tomatoes break down and the mixture becomes saucy, about 3 minutes. Add the beans, vegetable broth, honey, and cilantro and bring to a simmer. Turn the heat to low and simmer until the sauce thickens, about 3 minutes.

3. Crack the eggs and slide them gently out of their shells and into the sauce, leaving enough space in between them so they can cook evenly. Transfer the pan to the oven and bake until the whites are set but the yolks are still runny, about 4 minutes. For firmer yolks, bake a few minutes longer, checking for doneness every minute or so.

4. Meanwhile, wrap the tortillas in a kitchen towel and warm in the microwave for 30 seconds. Keep them wrapped until serving.

5. Place the warmed tortillas on heated plates. With a large spoon or spatula, carefully place the cooked eggs and sauce on top of the tortillas. Sprinkle with queso fresco and cilantro. Serve hot.

It's that easy: Roll the eggs and sauce up in the warm corn tortillas and eat them like a burrito (like my husband), or leave them open-faced and eat with a knife and fork (like me).

Extra hungry? Add another egg or two or add some tortilla chips for dipping.

In the glass: Beer just tastes great with Mexican food, I'm a fan of a longneck Corona Light with a twist of lime.

Migas

If you aren't from the Southwest, you may not know that migas is *the* antidote to a big night on the town. It's guaranteed to make you feel better after a little too much cerveza. But did you know that migas is also the antidote to a rough day at work? Comforting and yet stimulating at the same time, this dish of bell pepper, chile, tomatoes, eggs, and corn tortillas has what it takes to make whatever ails us fade quietly into the distance.

2 Tbsp olive oil	*2 garlic cloves, minced*
Four 6-in [15-cm] corn tortillas	*1 serrano chile, seeded and minced*
1 onion, diced	*½ cup [120 ml] vegetable broth, plus more as needed*
1 poblano chile, seeded and diced	*4 eggs*
1 red bell pepper, seeded, deribbed, and diced	*2 Tbsp milk*
½ tsp chili powder	*2 Tbsp minced fresh cilantro*
Kosher salt and freshly ground black pepper	*2 oz [55 g] Cotija or grated Monterey Jack cheese*
3 plum tomatoes, diced	*Hot sauce for serving*

1. Heat a 12-in [30.5-cm] skillet over medium-high heat, and add the olive oil. When the oil shimmers, add two of the tortillas and fry them until crispy, about 1 minute per side. Transfer the tortillas to a paper towel–lined plate. Repeat with the remaining tortillas. Set aside.

2. Add the onion, poblano, bell pepper, chili powder, ½ tsp salt, and a few grinds of pepper to the hot pan. Sauté until the vegetables begin to soften, about 3 minutes. Add the tomatoes, garlic, and serrano and sauté until the tomatoes start to break down, about 1 minute. Add the vegetable broth (it will spatter) and cook, stirring, until the vegetables are tender but still have a little bite, 2 minutes longer. If the broth evaporates and the vegetables are still tough, add more broth and cook a few minutes longer. The mixture should be saucy but not brothy.

3. In a medium bowl, whisk together the eggs, milk, ¼ tsp salt, and a few grinds of pepper.

4. Cut the tortillas into bite-size pieces and stir them into the sauce. Once they've warmed up, pour the eggs evenly over the top and, with a spatula, gently fold them into the sauce. Continue to fold the eggs into the sauce, allowing the uncooked eggs to flow to the bottom of the pan. Cook until the eggs set, about 1 minute longer. Stir in the cilantro.

5. Transfer the migas to heated plates. Sprinkle with cheese and serve with hot sauce on the side.

It's that easy: Poblanos are a fruity dark green chile that have just a touch of heat. Serrano chiles are long, skinny, and dark green, with medium to hot heat. I prefer serranos over jalapeños because they contain a more reliable sizzle.

Extra hungry? Add another egg or two to the mix.

In the glass: For dinner, I want a beer. For brunch, I want a Bloody Mary. You choose.

CHAPTER

3

Garden-Fresh Dinners

Mushrooms

with POLENTA and TALEGGIO

As a young man in West Virginia, my dad ate mush. My Oklahoman mama ate grits. When my husband and I recently ate this polenta for dinner, we realized it's basically the same cornmeal porridge my parents ate back in the '30s . . . but with a twist. This creamy comfort food is rich with butter, a touch of cream, and Parmesan cheese but the mushrooms are the star of the show. With their faux-meaty goodliness sprinkled through with shallot, Taleggio cheese, and a drizzle of truffle oil, this one-pan meal is a showstopper on a cool fall night. Thank you to Yotam Ottolenghi's *Plenty* for the inspiration for this dish.

4 Tbsp [55 g] unsalted butter

1 large shallot, minced

6 oz [170 g] mixed wild mushrooms, thinly sliced

Kosher salt and freshly ground black pepper

¼ cup [60 ml] white wine

2 Tbsp minced fresh tarragon

2 Tbsp minced fresh parsley

2⅓ cups [560 ml] vegetable broth

½ cup [70 g] quick-cooking polenta

3 Tbsp heavy cream

½ cup [15 g] grated Parmesan cheese

4 oz [115 g] Taleggio cheese, thinly sliced

Truffle oil for drizzling (optional)

1. Heat a 12-in [30.5-cm] oven-safe skillet over medium-high heat, and melt 2 Tbsp of the butter. When the butter sizzles, add the shallot and sauté until it begins to soften, about 1 minute. Add the mushrooms and a pinch of salt and pepper and sauté, stirring, until the mushrooms begin to soften, 3 to 4 minutes. Add the wine and cook until it almost completely evaporates, while stirring up all the good flavor on the bottom of the pan back into the mushrooms, about 2 minutes. Stir in 1 Tbsp of the tarragon and 1 Tbsp of the parsley. Taste and season with more salt and pepper, if it needs it. Transfer the mushrooms to a plate and keep warm.

2. Place an oven rack in the second highest position and preheat the broiler.

3. Add the vegetable broth to the hot skillet. Bring to a simmer over medium-high heat and slowly whisk in the polenta; it will begin to thicken immediately. Turn the heat to medium and cook, stirring, until the polenta thickens, about 5 minutes, then add the remaining 2 Tbsp butter, the cream, and Parmesan. Taste and season with more salt and pepper, if it needs it. Top the polenta with the Taleggio and place the skillet under the broiler until the cheese is melted and begins to brown, about 4 minutes. Top the polenta with the mushrooms and broil to reheat them, about 2 minutes. Sprinkle the remaining 1 Tbsp tarragon and 1 Tbsp parsley over the top of the mushrooms, drizzle with the truffle oil, if desired, and serve hot directly from the pan.

It's that easy: I rarely cook mushrooms without tossing in a minced shallot. The taste is milder than an onion, but it still gives the mushrooms a complex flavor base. Keep shallots within easy reach on your kitchen counter in the same place you keep a bulb of garlic.

Extra hungry? Pair it up with a crusty loaf of bread and olive oil for dipping and no one will leave the table hungry.

In the glass: A Côtes du Rhône from Georges Duboeuf will offset the richness and pair with this dish beautifully.

Italian Vegetables
and FRIED POLENTA CAKES

We've all seen those logs of polenta in the grocery store, but most of us don't know what to do with them. This is what you do with a log of polenta. You fry it up with cheese and fresh vegetables and eat like an Italian. *Mangia!*

¼ cup [35 g] all-purpose flour

Eight ½-in [12-mm] slices precooked polenta

2 Tbsp olive oil

½ cup [15 g] grated Parmesan cheese

½ red onion, thinly sliced

4 cups [150 g] thinly sliced rapini

1 small red bell pepper, seeded, deribbed, and thinly sliced

1 small head fennel, halved, cored, and thinly sliced

Kosher salt and freshly ground black pepper

1 cup [140 g] grape tomatoes

Leaves from 4 sprigs fresh oregano, chopped

1 garlic clove, minced

2 tsp balsamic vinegar

1. Put the flour in a shallow bowl. Pat the polenta rounds dry with a paper towel, dredge them in the flour, and shake off the excess.

2. Heat a 12-in [30.5-cm] skillet over medium-high heat, and add 1 Tbsp of the olive oil. When the oil shimmers, add the polenta rounds in batches and cook until crispy and lightly browned on both sides, 5 to 6 minutes. Top four of the polenta rounds with half of the Parmesan and then cover with the remaining rounds (the Parmesan will melt and act as a kind of glue to hold them together). Immediately transfer the polenta to a plate and keep warm.

3. Add the remaining 1 Tbsp olive oil to the hot skillet. Add the onion and sauté until it begins to soften, about 2 minutes. Add the rapini, bell pepper, fennel, ½ tsp salt, and a few grinds of pepper and sauté the vegetables, stirring, until they soften, about 5 minutes. Add the tomatoes, oregano, and garlic and cook, stirring, until the tomatoes pop and become juicy, about 3 minutes. Stir in the vinegar. Taste and season with more salt and pepper, if it needs it.

4. Arrange the polenta on heated plates and top with the hot vegetables and remaining Parmesan. Serve hot.

It's that easy: *Rapini is also called broccoli rabe. The tips resemble broccoli but it has many more leaves and much narrower stems. Its lightly bitter taste pairs well with the fried polenta, sweet vegetables, and salty cheese in this dish.*

Extra hungry? *Cook a few additional rounds of polenta and increase the Parmesan cheese to ⅔ cup [20 g].*

In the glass: *A Pinot Grigio from Santa Margherita takes this weeknight meal to the weekend.*

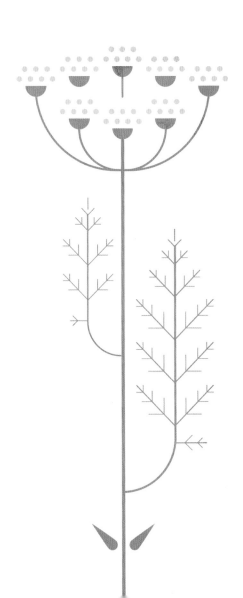

Moussaka

Where I come from, moussaka is what you make in the late summer when all the neighbors' gardens are prolific with eggplant, zucchini, and tomatoes. I like to serve this homey dish hot or at room temperature and pile it on top of toasted country-style bread. The Kefalotyri is a hard sheep's-milk cheese from Greece. It can be difficult to find, but Parmesan is a great substitute.

1 small eggplant, peeled and cut into slices a little less than ¹/₂ in [12 mm] thick

Kosher salt and freshly ground black pepper

4 Tbsp [60 ml] olive oil, plus more as needed

1 onion, chopped

One 6-in [15-cm] zucchini, halved lengthwise and thinly sliced

2 garlic cloves, minced

1 ripe tomato, peeled, quartered, seeded, and chopped

1 Tbsp balsamic vinegar

¹/₄ tsp ground cinnamon

¹/₄ cup [8 g] grated Kefalotyri or Parmesan cheese

Toasted country-style bread slices for serving

1. Preheat the oven to 350°F [180°C].

2. Season the eggplant slices with salt and pepper.

3. Heat a 12-in [30.5-cm] oven-safe skillet or 3-qt [2.8-L] Dutch oven over medium-high heat, and add 2 Tbsp of the olive oil. When the oil shimmers, add half of the eggplant slices and cook until limp and lightly browned on both sides, about 5 minutes. Transfer the eggplant to a plate, add the remaining 2 Tbsp olive oil to the pan, and cook the remaining eggplant in the same way.

4. Add the onion, zucchini, and ¹/₄ tsp salt to the hot skillet and sauté until the vegetables soften, about 4 minutes. Add the garlic, tomato, vinegar, and cinnamon and cook until the tomato gives off its juices, about 4 minutes. Taste and season with more salt and pepper, if it needs it. Spread the vegetables evenly in the pan, arrange the eggplant slices on top, and sprinkle with the Kefalotyri.

5. Transfer the pan to the oven and bake until the top is crispy and the flavors have blended, about 15 minutes.

continued

6. Arrange the bread on heated plates, spoon the moussaka over the bread, and serve hot or at room temperature.

It's that easy: *Though moussaka is delicious year-round, try to make it in the summer, when you can get really fresh tomatoes and zucchini. Every year, I'm amazed by the superior taste of fresh summertime produce.*

Extra hungry? *Make a few indentations in the tomato mixture, break eggs into them, and sprinkle the eggs with a little salt and pepper. Top with the eggplant and bake as directed. The eggs will be hard-cooked underneath the eggplant, but they'll taste great all mashed up with the tomatoey vegetables and cheese.*

In the glass: *Vinho verde is a slightly fizzy white wine from Portugal. Serve it really cold, as you would a Sauvignon Blanc.*

Fried Eggplant Stacks

with BUFFALO MOZZARELLA, CHERMOULA, *and* PINE NUTS

A blend of Italian and North African flavors, these stacks of fried eggplant and fresh mozzarella topped with a spicy green sauce are refreshingly familiar, yet new. A Tunisian sauce used to flavor fish and vegetables, chermoula is often made with a mix of herbs, lemon, oil, garlic, cumin, and red bell peppers.

---

¹/₃ cup [10 g] coarsely chopped fresh flat-leaf parsley

¹/₃ cup [10 g] coarsely chopped fresh cilantro leaves and tender stems

2 garlic cloves, minced

¹/₂ tsp paprika

1 Tbsp fresh lemon juice

7 Tbsp [110 ml] olive oil

¹/₄ tsp ground cumin

Pinch of red pepper flakes

Kosher salt

¹/₄ cup [35 g] all-purpose flour

1¹/₄ cups [75 g] panko bread crumbs

1 egg

1 medium eggplant, trimmed and cut into twelve ¹/₂-in [12-mm] rounds

Freshly ground black pepper

6 oz [170 g] fresh buffalo mozzarella cheese, cut into 6 slices

2 jarred roasted red bell peppers, cut into 3 pieces each

3 Tbsp pine nuts

---

1. Preheat the oven to 375°F [190°C].

2. In a small bowl, stir together the parsley, cilantro, garlic, paprika, lemon juice, 3 Tbsp of the olive oil, the cumin, red pepper flakes, and ¹/₄ tsp salt. Set the chermoula aside.

3. Put the flour and panko into two separate shallow bowls. Beat the egg and 2 Tbsp water in a third shallow bowl.

4. Season the eggplant slices with salt and black pepper, dredge them in the flour, and shake off the excess. Dip in the egg, then coat well with the panko. Set aside on a cutting board or sheet pan.

continued

5. Heat a 12-in [30.5-cm] oven-safe skillet over medium-high heat, and add 2 Tbsp olive oil. When the oil shimmers, add six of the eggplant slices and cook until browned and tender on both sides, about 4 minutes. Transfer the eggplant to a plate. Add the remaining 2 Tbsp olive oil to the pan and cook the remaining six eggplant slices in the same way.

6. Dollop 1 Tbsp or so of the chermoula on the eggplant in the pan and top with a slice of mozzarella and a piece of roasted red pepper. Cover with the reserved eggplant slices.

7. Transfer the pan to the oven and bake the eggplant stacks until almost warmed through, about 15 minutes, then dollop with another 1 Tbsp or so of the remaining chermoula and sprinkle the pine nuts over the top. Return to the oven and bake until completely warmed through and the pine nuts are browned, about 5 minutes longer.

8. Serve hot on heated plates.

It's that easy: In Morocco, they use chermoula to flavor meat, fish, and vegetables, but here we're using it to flavor breaded and fried eggplant stacks, which might be more Italian than Moroccan. The eggplant stacks definitely benefit from Morocco's zingy green sauce, so make up a double batch in the summer to add extra zip to easy grilled dinners.

Extra hungry? Add some sliced tomatoes drizzled with balsamic vinegar and sprinkled with salt and pepper to serve alongside the eggplant stacks.

In the glass: I like a white wine with the spicy chermoula. The crisp acidity of Sauvignon Blanc cuts through the rich breading on these stacks. Look for a bottle from Oyster Bay.

Eggplant Rollatini

If you like eggplant Parmesan, you're going to love eggplant rollatini. Picture fried eggplant rolled into a tidy bundle with a secret center of ricotta cheese. In case you didn't know, eggplant Parmesan doesn't have a hidden center of cheese. Nope. No cheese in the center.

1 medium eggplant, peeled and cut lengthwise into 6 long slices between ¼ in [6 mm] and ½ in [12 mm] thick

Kosher salt and freshly ground black pepper

2 Tbsp olive oil, plus more as needed

⅔ cup [160 g] whole-milk ricotta cheese

½ cup [40 g] shredded mozzarella cheese

¼ cup [8 g] grated Parmesan cheese

3 Tbsp chopped fresh basil

1 egg yolk

1 cup [240 ml] marinara sauce

½ lemon, cut into 4 wedges

1. Preheat the oven to 350°F [180°C].

2. Season the eggplant slices with salt and pepper.

3. Heat a 12-in [30.5-cm] skillet over medium-high heat, and add the 2 Tbsp olive oil. When the oil shimmers, add the eggplant in batches, adding more oil if necessary, and fry until browned on both sides and softened, about 4 minutes. Transfer the eggplant to a plate.

4. In a small bowl, stir together the ricotta, mozzarella, Parmesan, 2 Tbsp of the basil, the egg yolk, and a pinch of salt and pepper.

5. Working with one slice of eggplant at a time, spread about ¼ cup [40 g] of the cheese mixture evenly over the eggplant. Starting from the narrow end, roll up the eggplant slices, enclosing the cheese filling. Arrange the rollatinis in the skillet seam-side down and top with the marinara sauce.

6. Transfer the pan to the oven and bake the rollatinis until warmed through, about 20 minutes.

7. Place the rollatinis on heated plates and sprinkle with the remaining 1 Tbsp basil. Serve hot with the lemon on the side for squeezing.

It's that easy: *The first and last slices of the egg-plant will not be easy to work with, as they each have a rounded side that won't brown well. Cut them into sticks and fry them up as an appetizer, or throw them into your next pasta dish.*

Extra hungry: *A salad would be refreshing. How about some cucumbers, sliced up and tossed with a sprinkle of white wine vinegar and a glug of olive oil?*

In the glass: *A Sangiovese or Chianti would be delish. Look for the word "riserva" on the label, as it denotes a higher-quality wine that has aged a little longer. Try a bottle from Ruffino for a good value.*

Vadouvan-Spiced Cabbage

with TOFU

I am a cabbage lover. I admit it, freely. I love cabbage cooked many ways, but it's especially tasty when flavored with vadouvan, crunchy almonds, and browned tofu. Even if cabbage has never been your favorite vegetable, you'll be amazed at how delicious it can be when sautéed with onion, garlic, spices, and ginger.

½ cup [70 g] all-purpose flour

6 oz [170 g] firm tofu, cut in half and then into ¼-in [6-mm] slices, patted dry

2 Tbsp vegetable oil

2 Tbsp unsalted butter

1 small onion, thinly sliced

2 garlic cloves, minced

One 2-in [5-cm] knob fresh ginger, peeled and minced

2 tsp vadouvan or curry powder

¼ tsp red pepper flakes

1 small head cabbage, cored and thinly sliced

Kosher salt

½ cup [70 g] frozen peas, thawed

Freshly ground black pepper

¼ cup [30 g] chopped salted almonds

1 Tbsp minced fresh flat-leaf parsley

---

1. Put the flour in a shallow bowl. Dredge the tofu in the flour and shake off the excess.

2. Heat a 12-in [30.5-cm] skillet over medium-high heat, and add the vegetable oil. When the oil shimmers, add the tofu and cook until lightly golden on both sides, about 4 minutes. Transfer the tofu to a paper towel–lined plate.

3. Melt the butter in the hot pan. When the butter sizzles, add the onion, garlic, ginger, vadouvan, and red pepper flakes. Sauté until the onion begins to soften, about 2 minutes. Add the cabbage and ½ tsp salt and sauté until the cabbage is tender, about 5 minutes. Stir in the peas and tofu and cook for another minute to heat them through. Taste and season with black pepper and more salt, if it needs it.

4. Transfer the cabbage to heated plates and sprinkle the almonds and parsley on top. Serve hot.

It's that easy: *Vadouvan is a Frenchified curry powder with added shallot and garlic flavors. It isn't always easy to find in grocery stores, but it's worth seeking out if you're a curry lover who wants to try something new. Vadouvan has a smoky-sweet flavor that's not found in most commercial curry blends.*

Extra hungry? *Though you may have to cook it in two batches, you can always brown up extra tofu.*

In the glass: *The lemon-lime and herbal flavors of Indaba Chenin Blanc are perfect with this spicy dish.*

Roasted Brussels Sprouts

with BUTTERNUT SQUASH, APPLE, *and* WALNUTS

For some reason, this is the dish that all my recipe testers wanted to make. Is it the roasted Brussels sprouts? Or is it the combination of browned sprouts and butternut squash, apple, and walnuts? You decide.

---

8 oz [230 g] Brussels sprouts, trimmed and quartered

10 oz [280 g] butternut squash, peeled and cut into ½-in [12-mm] chunks

1 Honeycrisp apple, peeled and cut into 1-in [2.5-cm] chunks

2 medium shallots, coarsely chopped

Leaves from 2 sprigs fresh rosemary, chopped

2 Tbsp unsalted butter, melted

1 Tbsp pure maple syrup

Kosher salt and freshly ground black pepper

One 15-oz [425-g] can butter beans or cannellini beans, drained and rinsed

½ cup [60 g] chopped walnuts

¼ cup [50 g] dried cranberries, soaked in ¼ cup [60 ml] hot water for 5 minutes then drained

1 Tbsp minced fresh flat-leaf parsley

---

1. Preheat the oven to 425°F [220°C]. Line a sheet pan with parchment paper.

2. In a large bowl, toss together the Brussels sprouts, butternut squash, apple, shallots, and rosemary. Pour the melted butter and maple syrup over the top and season with ½ tsp salt and a few grinds of pepper. Toss until the fruit and vegetables are evenly coated in the butter and syrup. Spread the fruit and vegetables evenly on the prepared sheet pan.

3. Roast until the fruit and vegetables begin to soften, about 15 minutes, then toss again with a spatula. Roast until the sprouts and squash are browned and tender, about 10 minutes longer. Add the butter beans and walnuts and roast until warmed through, about 5 minutes.

4. Remove the sheet pan from the oven and toss the cranberries with the roasted fruit and vegetables. Taste and season with more salt and pepper, if it needs it.

continued

5. Transfer the roasted fruit and vegetables to heated plates and sprinkle with the parsley. Serve hot.

It's that easy: Roasting fruits and vegetables is a simple business, but the timing can be inexact. There are many variables, from the heat of your oven to the freshness of the produce, that will translate to your dish cooking for a longer or shorter time. Use the recommended cooking times as a guide, and check frequently for the best results.

Extra hungry? Slip roasted fruit and vegetables into pita pockets and enjoy a warm sandwich.

In the glass: The Italian grape verdicchio has been called the thinking person's Pinot Grigio. Citrusy but with playful minerality, verdicchio works with many dishes. Look for a bottle from Marchetti.

START TO FINISH
35 minutes
. . .
HANDS-ON TIME
30 minutes
. . .
Serves 2

General Tso's Bok Choy

with TOFU

When the kids were young, our family used to order General Tso's chicken from our local Chinese takeout. The chicken part wasn't always great, but I loved the sauce, which is delicious, by the way, with crunchy bok choy.

Sauce	*¼ cup [35 g] all-purpose flour*
2 Tbsp soy sauce	*8 oz [230 g] firm tofu, cut into ¼-in [6-mm] slices and patted dry*
2 Tbsp rice vinegar	
2 Tbsp sugar	*3 Tbsp vegetable oil*
2 Tbsp hoisin	*1 onion, thinly sliced*
1 Tbsp mirin	*One 2-in [5-cm] knob fresh ginger, peeled and minced*
1 tsp chile-garlic sauce	*2 garlic cloves, minced*
2 tsp cornstarch	*1 large head bok choy, thinly sliced*
1 tsp dark sesame oil	*½ red bell pepper, seeded, deribbed, and thinly sliced*
2 Tbsp water	*1 cup [100 g] snow peas*
Freshly ground black pepper	*1 green onion, white and green parts, thinly sliced*
	Cooked rice for serving

1. To make the sauce: In a small bowl, stir together the soy sauce, rice vinegar, sugar, hoisin, mirin, chile-garlic sauce, cornstarch, sesame oil, water, and a few grinds of black pepper. Set aside.

2. Put the flour in a shallow bowl. Dredge the tofu in the flour and shake off the excess.

3. Heat a 12-in [30.5-cm] skillet or wok over medium-high heat, and add 2 Tbsp of the vegetable oil. When the oil shimmers, add the tofu and cook until lightly golden on both sides, about 4 minutes. Transfer the tofu to a paper towel–lined plate.

continued

4. Add the remaining 1 Tbsp vegetable oil and the onion, ginger, and garlic to the hot pan and sauté until fragrant, about 1 minute. Add the bok choy, bell pepper, and snow peas and cook, stirring, until the vegetables begin to soften, about 3 minutes. Add the sauce (it will sizzle) and cook, tossing the vegetables until completely coated with the sauce, about 1 minute. Stir in the tofu and heat another minute or so to warm everything evenly. Sprinkle with the green onion.

5. Transfer the tofu and bok choy to bowls and serve hot, with rice alongside.

It's that easy: *I know there are lots of Chinese ingredients here, but my local grocery stocks them all. You will use them again, and they last forever in the fridge. Rice vinegar is great in salad dressings. Hoisin is Chinese barbecue sauce and can be used the same way. Mirin can be used to season soups and stews. Chile-garlic sauce spices up soups and stews. Sesame oil is great in salad dressing or lightly drizzled over cooked vegetables.*

Extra hungry? *Add some additional tofu. About 4 oz [115 g] should do it.*

In the glass: *Riesling goes beautifully with Chinese flavors. Look for a bottle of Chateau Ste. Michelle Harvest Select Riesling from the Columbia Valley.*

....
START TO FINISH
50 minutes
...
HANDS-ON TIME
15 minutes
...
Serves 2
....

Baked Sweet Potatoes

with BLACK BEANS and SPINACH

Okay, I know. A baked sweet potato for dinner isn't really dinner. But when you add black beans, along with spinach and sweet-tart grape tomatoes, it becomes a meal. If you haven't had a baked sweet potato in a while, you might have forgotten how good it can taste. Trust me, you'll remember quickly.

---

2 large sweet potatoes

2 Tbsp olive oil

2 green onions, white and green parts, thinly sliced

1 garlic clove, minced

5 oz [140 g] baby spinach

1 cup [140 g] grape tomatoes, halved

1 cup [220 g] canned black beans, drained and rinsed

Kosher salt and freshly ground black pepper

2 tsp fresh lemon juice

2 Tbsp minced fresh cilantro

---

1. Preheat the oven to 375°F [190°C].

2. Rub the sweet potatoes with 1 Tbsp of the olive oil. Poke the potatoes with a fork in a few places so that steam can escape.

3. Heat a 12-in [30.5 cm] oven-safe skillet over medium-high heat. When the skillet is hot, lay the sweet potatoes in the pan. Transfer the skillet to the oven and roast until the sweet potatoes are soft and wrinkly, about 45 minutes. Remove the skillet from the oven and transfer the sweet potatoes to two heated plates.

4. Add the remaining 1 Tbsp olive oil to the hot pan (careful, the handle's hot) and warm over medium-high heat. When the oil shimmers, add the green onions and garlic and sauté until the green onions begin to soften, about 30 seconds. Add the spinach and cook, tossing it until it wilts, about 2 minutes. Add the tomatoes, black beans, 1/4 tsp salt, and a few grinds of pepper and cook, tossing until warmed through, about 1 minute. Stir in the lemon juice and cilantro.

5. Cut the sweet potatoes in half lengthwise, leaving the bottom intact, and press the ends together so that a "bowl" is created for the bean mixture. Season the sweet potatoes with salt and pepper and top with the black bean mixture. It won't all fit inside the potato but that's okay. Serve hot.

It's that easy: Sweet potatoes are one of the most nutritious foods you can eat for dinner. Full of beta-carotene and vitamin A, they become a complete meal when paired with protein-packed black beans and iron-rich spinach. Look out, Popeye. This low-fat, nutritious dinner is so good that it just might make it into the regular rotation.

Extra hungry? Make a quick and easy garlic toast. Just drizzle a couple slices of sourdough with olive oil, toast them, and then rub them with a garlic clove.

In the glass: I like Chardonnay with sweet potatoes. Look for Edna Valley Vineyard Paragon Chardonnay for a tasty bottle that will pair with a variety of foods.

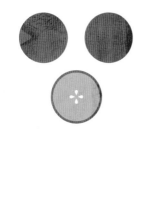

Sweet Potato Cakes

with APPLE and SPINACH

These crispy sweet potato cakes are usually topped with applesauce, but for dinner I like to top them with a spinach salad coated in a warm appley dressing. It adds just the right amount of tart to these sweet and crispy little rounds.

1 onion, diced

1 cup [230 g] firmly packed peeled and grated sweet potato

½ cup [120 g] firmly packed peeled and grated russet potato

1 egg

3 Tbsp all-purpose flour

¼ tsp baking powder

Pinch of freshly grated nutmeg

Kosher salt and freshly ground black pepper

2 Tbsp vegetable oil

2 Tbsp white balsamic vinegar

2 Tbsp olive oil

2 Crispin, Braeburn, or other crisp, sweet apples, peeled and diced

2 oz [55 g] baby spinach

1. In a medium bowl, stir together the onion, sweet potato, russet potato, and egg. Stir in the flour, baking powder, nutmeg, ½ tsp salt, and a few grinds of pepper just until combined.

2. Heat a 12-in [30.5-cm] skillet over medium heat, and add the vegetable oil. When the oil shimmers, drop the potato batter into the skillet in four equal mounds. Using the back of a fork or a spatula, press the tops and sides to make the mounds neat and compact, about 4 in [10 cm] wide. Cook, without disturbing, until the bottoms brown, about 4 minutes. Using a thin spatula, carefully flip the pancakes to brown the second side, flattening the tops gently with the spatula. Cook until the

second side is browned and the pancakes are cooked through, about 4 minutes. Transfer the pancakes to heated plates.

3. Remove the pan from the heat and let it cool for a few minutes. Off the heat, add the vinegar, olive oil, and apple (it will spatter) to the skillet (it will still be hot) and stir it around until the apples warm up.

4. Mound the spinach on top of the pancakes and pour the hot dressing and apples over the top. Season with salt and pepper. Serve hot.

It's that easy: One of my favorite kitchen tools is a fish spatula. I love it because it has a very thin edge and makes flipping delicate pancakes a breeze. Pick up one the next time you're in a cookware store. You'll be glad you did.

Extra hungry? Add another apple, a little more vinegar to the dressing, and another handful or two of spinach to the plates.

In the glass: Apple cider or, if you're of a certain mind, a glass of hard cider will soften the edges of your day.

Latkes

with RUTABAGA, RAPINI, *and* PARMESAN

I could wax rhapsodic over the many ways I love a potato pancake, but lacing the pancake with rutabaga is pure genius, if I do say so myself. When paired with rapini and cheese, it's the proverbial party in your mouth.

2 cups [500 g] peeled and grated Yukon gold potato	*Kosher salt and freshly ground black pepper*
1 cup [250 g] peeled and grated rutabaga	*3 Tbsp olive oil*
1 onion, finely chopped	*1 bunch rapini, trimmed and chopped*
1 egg, beaten	*2 garlic cloves, minced*
2 Tbsp all-purpose flour	*½ lemon*
½ tsp chopped fresh thyme	*Shaved Parmesan cheese for garnish*
Pinch of freshly grated nutmeg	*¼ cup [30 g] chopped salted almonds, toasted*

1. In a large bowl, toss together the potato, rutabaga, onion, egg, flour, thyme, nutmeg, ½ tsp salt, and a few grinds of pepper.

2. Heat a 12-in [30.5-cm] skillet over medium-high heat, and add 2 Tbsp of the olive oil. When the oil shimmers, drop the potato-rutabaga batter into the skillet in four equal mounds. Using the back of a fork or a spatula, press the tops and sides to make the mounds neat and compact, about 5 in [12 cm] wide. Cook, without disturbing, until the bottoms brown and the pancakes firm up, about 3 minutes. Using a thin spatula, carefully flip the latkes to brown the second side, flattening the tops

gently with the spatula. Cook until the second side is browned and the latkes are cooked through, about 3 minutes. Transfer the latkes to heated plates.

3. Add the remaining 1 Tbsp olive oil to the hot pan. When the oil shimmers, add the rapini and season with salt and pepper. Cook the rapini, tossing it until it wilts, about 2 minutes. Add the garlic and cook, tossing the rapini again so it cooks evenly, about 1 minute longer. Squeeze the lemon over the rapini and toss to coat. Turn off the heat.

continued

4. Top the latkes with the rapini and scatter Parmesan and the almonds over. Serve hot.

It's that easy: If your potatoes exude a lot of liquid when grated, squeeze some of it out before mixing with the other ingredients. That way, the latkes will crisp up more nicely—crunchy latkes are a must.

Extra hungry? Potato pancakes are pretty full of carbs, but if you want to lighten them up you could scatter some diced tomato tossed with balsamic vinegar, salt, and pepper over the top. It will add a little color too.

In the glass: You could drink anything with this meal. I like to celebrate with a lighter-bodied Pinot Noir from Hahn Estates on California's Central Coast.

START TO FINISH
70 minutes
...
HANDS-ON TIME
25 minutes
...
Serves 2
....

Potato Gratin

with TOMATO, OLIVE, *and* CAPERS

A potato gratin can be a pretty quick meal if you slice the potatoes thinly and jump-start the cooking on the stove top. My way of turning this side dish into a complete meal is to add rosemary and then top with tomato, salty capers, and olives (kind of like a salad). This gratin is also made with broth instead of cream, so it's a little more forgiving to your waistline. If you have a mandoline or Benriner slicer, use it to thinly slice the potatoes.

2 Tbsp unsalted butter

1 onion, thinly sliced

1 tsp chopped fresh rosemary

Kosher salt and freshly ground black pepper

1½ lb [680 g] boiling potatoes, peeled and thinly sliced

1 cup [240 ml] vegetable broth

1 garlic clove, minced

1 tomato, thinly sliced

8 pitted Kalamata olives, chopped

1 tsp capers, rinsed and chopped

½ cup [50 g] grated Gruyère or Swiss cheese

1. Preheat the oven to 375°F [190°C].

2. Heat a 12-in [30.5-cm] skillet over medium heat, and melt the butter. When the butter sizzles, add the onion, rosemary, ¼ tsp salt, and a few grinds of pepper. Sauté until the onion softens, about 3 minutes. Add the potatoes, vegetable broth, garlic, ¼ tsp salt, and a few grinds of pepper; stir to combine; and bring to a simmer. Turn the heat to low, cover, and simmer for 10 minutes.

3. Uncover the pan and transfer to the oven. Bake until some of the broth has been absorbed and the potatoes are almost tender, about 15 minutes. Remove the gratin from the oven and top with the tomato, olives, capers, a few grinds of pepper, and the cheese. Return to the oven and bake until the cheese is bubbly and the potatoes are tender, about 15 minutes.

continued

4. Remove the gratin from the oven and let sit for 10 minutes. Cut into wedges and serve on heated plates.

It's that easy: *Capers come either in brine or packed in salt. I prefer salt-packed capers, as they have a firmer texture. However, they must be rinsed well in a few changes of water to remove the salt. The brined capers can be used straight from the jar.*

Extra hungry? *This hot meal deserves a little green. Toss up a salad with a little escarole, cut-up navel orange, and a couple of olives. Drizzle with white balsamic vinegar and a glug of olive oil.*

In the glass: *I like a white wine with good acidity to break down the starch of the gratin. Look for a Sauvignon Blanc from Benziger for a zingy bottle with good value.*

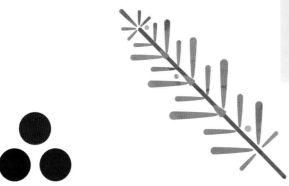

Roasted Cauliflower Gratin

with RYE CROUTON

Back when I used to teach at a cooking school, I made a roasted cauliflower gratin with cream sauce and Gruyère that was always a hit with students. This version uses a custard instead of the usual cream sauce and, since it's meant for dinner, I added some bitter radicchio to balance out all the sweetness from the cauliflower and dairy. I'm so glad I thought of the rye crouton to go underneath. It adds heft to the dish while sopping up all that creamy goodness. Whatever you do, don't forget the crouton!

2 eggs, beaten	*1 onion, diced*
1 tsp Dijon mustard	*½ head cauliflower, trimmed and thinly sliced*
½ cup [120 ml] heavy cream	*1 garlic clove, minced*
½ cup [120 ml] milk	*1 small head radicchio, cored and thinly sliced*
Pinch of freshly grated nutmeg	*3 oz [85 g] fontina cheese, grated*
Kosher salt and freshly ground black pepper	*2 slices country-style rye or multigrain bread, toasted*
1 Tbsp olive oil	

1. Place an oven rack in the second highest position and preheat the broiler.

2. In a medium bowl, whisk together the eggs and mustard, followed by the cream, milk, nutmeg, ½ tsp salt, and a few grinds of pepper. Set aside.

3. Heat a 12-in [30.5-cm] skillet over medium-high heat, and add the olive oil. When the oil shimmers, add the onion and cauliflower. Season with salt and pepper and sauté, stirring, until the vegetables begin to soften, about 4 minutes.

4. Transfer the skillet to the oven and broil the cauliflower for about 2 minutes, then toss and broil until the cauliflower is lightly browned in spots, about 2 minutes longer. Return the skillet to the stove top and set over medium-high heat. Turn off the broiler and set the oven temperature to 375°F [190°C].

5. Add the garlic and radicchio to the skillet and cook until the radicchio wilts, about 2 minutes. Spread the vegetables evenly in the skillet, sprinkle with the cheese, and pour the egg mixture evenly over the top. Return the skillet to the oven and bake until the custard sets, about 10 minutes.

6. Remove the gratin from the oven and let sit for 5 minutes. Place a slice of toasted rye on each of two heated plates. Cut the gratin into wedges and place on the toasts. Serve hot.

It's that easy: It's important that the cauliflower is cut thinly so that it cooks quickly. I usually quarter the cauliflower half and then slice each quarter thinly. Little bits will shard off from the stems. Just scrape them into the pan with the slices. They will all cook up fine.

Extra hungry? Make an open-face sandwich to go on the side. Just slather a slice of rye bread with unsalted butter, top with very thinly sliced peppery radishes, and sprinkle with salt and pepper.

In the glass: Search out 3 Brooms Sauvignon Blanc from Marlborough, New Zealand, as it comes up in many a wine expert's best-buy column. Or you could opt for a Pinot Noir from Castle Rock.

Celery Root and Yukon Gold Gratin

with SWISS CHARD and GORGONZOLA

If you've never combined celery root with potatoes, you're in for a treat. The celery-like herbal notes from the knobby root elevate this potato dish to a new level, and the Swiss chard adds a welcome touch of green. While tasty, the greens also cut the richness of the dish just enough to ease any guilt you may have for eating something so delicious on a work night.

1 Tbsp unsalted butter

1 shallot, finely chopped

½ tsp minced fresh thyme

1 bunch Swiss chard, ribs and leaves separated and coarsely chopped

1 tsp Dijon mustard

1 cup [240 ml] heavy cream

½ cup [120 ml] milk

1 large Yukon gold potato, peeled and very thinly sliced

1 small celery root, peeled and very thinly sliced

Kosher salt and freshly ground black pepper

4 oz [115 g] crumbled Gorgonzola

1. Preheat the oven to 375°F [190°C].

2. Heat a 12-in [30.5-cm] oven-proof skillet over medium-high heat, and melt the butter. When the butter sizzles, add the shallot and thyme. Cook until the shallot softens, about 1 minute. Add the chard ribs and cook until they begin to soften, about 2 minutes. Add the chard leaves by the handful, letting them wilt before adding more. Cook until the leaves are tender, about 2 minutes. Add the mustard, cream, milk, potato, celery root, ½ tsp salt, and a few grinds of pepper, stirring to combine. Turn the heat to medium and cook until the vegetables are warmed through and the liquid

begins to bubble, about 3 minutes. Sprinkle the Gorgonzola over the top and press the vegetables down into the liquid so that they cook nicely.

3. Cover the skillet with aluminum foil, transfer to the oven, and bake until the potato is almost tender, about 30 minutes. Remove the foil and bake until the potato is tender, the sauce has thickened, and the top is browned, about 20 minutes longer. To test, poke the gratin with the tip of a sharp knife. If it slides in easily with no resistance, it's done.

4. Remove the gratin from the oven and let sit for 5 minutes. Cut into wedges and serve on heated plates.

It's that easy: *I started adding celery root to mashed potatoes about twenty years ago. I loved how the celery root made the potatoes even more savory, so I started adding them to potato casseroles as well. Other potato-friendly add-ins are turnips, parsnips, and rutabagas. Just be sure to cut them down to the same size as the potatoes so that they all cook at the same rate.*

Extra hungry? *You shouldn't be hungry after eating this hearty dish, but a salad can be a colorful and fresh accompaniment that also cuts through some of the gratin's richness. Scrub a few beets and shave them into ribbons with a vegetable peeler. Toss with a splash of lemon juice, a glug of olive oil, and sprinkles of salt, pepper, and parsley.*

In the glass: *A lusty Petite Sirah from California or a Shiraz from Australia are the same grape, just different names. Bogle makes a reasonably priced Petite Sirah and Layer Cake Shiraz from the Barossa Valley is also a good value.*

CHAPTER

4

Grains & Beans with Soul

Tabbouleh

with POMEGRANATE

Loads of fresh herbs and wholesome grains are what make this light salad so appealing. If you're not familiar with bulgur, it's toasted cracked wheat that plumps up in hot water in a matter of minutes, which makes this salad perfect for a last-minute dinner. Try eating it as they do in Lebanon, by scooping it up with crisp romaine lettuce leaves.

1¼ cups [300 ml] water

Kosher salt

1 cup [150 g] bulgur

⅓ cup [10 g] finely chopped fresh flat-leaf parsley

¼ cup [7 g] finely chopped fresh mint

2 green onions, green part only, finely chopped

1 cup [140 g] cherry tomatoes, halved

2 radishes, thinly sliced

½ cucumber, peeled, seeded, and diced

½ cup [80 g] pomegranate seeds

2 Tbsp fresh lemon juice, plus more as needed

3 Tbsp extra-virgin olive oil

¼ tsp ground cumin

Freshly ground black pepper

Romaine lettuce leaves for serving

1. In a 3-qt [2.8-L] saucepan over medium-high heat, bring the water to a boil. Add ½ tsp salt to the boiling water and pour in the bulgur. Stir, cover, turn off the heat, and let sit until the bulgur softens, about 15 minutes.

2. In a large bowl, combine the parsley, mint, green onions, tomatoes, radishes, cucumber, pomegranate seeds, lemon juice, olive oil, cumin, ¼ tsp salt, and a few grinds of pepper. Add the bulgur and toss together. Taste and season with more lemon juice, salt, and pepper, if it needs it.

3. Mound the tabbouleh on plates. Serve hot with romaine lettuce leaves for scooping.

It's that easy: *It's simple to get the seeds out of a pomegranate. Cut through the skin around the equator of the pomegranate and pry it in half with your fingers. Hold one half over a large bowl, cut-side down, and rap it with a wooden spoon, knocking the seeds from the white membrane. Some of the membrane will come out as well, but just pick it out from the ruby-red seeds and discard it along with the skin. Keep the seeds refrigerated in a sealed bag for up to 3 days.*

Extra hungry? *Toss a bit of feta cheese into the salad for a little protein punch.*

In the glass: *Look for a fairly dry white or rosé. We had this dish with a rosé from Tavel, my favorite summer quaff.*

Couscous

with BROCCOLINI, CHICKPEAS, *and* FRIED HALLOUMI

When you're looking for a really quick and easy meal, this is the one to cook. Couscous is notoriously fast, and Broccolini's slender stalks tenderize rapidly as well. Halloumi is a creamy semisoft cheese with a slightly salty flavor. When fried and combined with carrot, raisins, chickpeas, and cashews, this is the kind of stand-alone salad we look for when we need hot food quickly.

¼ *cup [35 g] all-purpose flour*

2 oz [55 g] halloumi cheese, cut into ¼-in [6-mm] slices

2 Tbsp olive oil

1 onion, diced

1 garlic clove, minced

1 bunch Broccolini, cut into bite-size pieces

½ red bell pepper, seeded, deribbed, and diced

1 carrot, grated

¼ *cup [40 g] golden raisins*

1½ cups [360 ml] vegetable broth

Kosher salt and freshly ground black pepper

¾ *cup [135 g] couscous*

1 cup [220 g] canned chickpeas, drained

2 tsp cider vinegar, plus more as needed

¼ *cup [30 g] chopped cashews*

2 Tbsp minced fresh flat-leaf parsley

1. Put the flour in a shallow bowl. Dredge the halloumi in the flour and shake off the excess.

2. Heat a 12-in [30.5-cm] skillet over medium-high heat, and add the olive oil. When the oil shimmers, add the halloumi and cook until browned on both sides, about 3 minutes. Transfer the halloumi to a plate and keep warm.

3. Add the onion to the hot skillet and sauté until it begins to soften, about 1 minute. Add the garlic, Broccolini, and bell pepper and sauté until the Broccolini turns bright green, about 2 minutes. Stir in the carrot, raisins, vegetable broth, ½ tsp salt, and a few grinds of pepper and bring to a boil. Quickly stir in the couscous and chickpeas, cover, and turn off the heat.

4. Let the couscous stand until it softens and the vegetables finish cooking, about 5 minutes. Fluff with a fork and drizzle with the vinegar. Taste and season with more salt, pepper, and vinegar, if it needs it. Stir in the cashews and parsley.

5. Scoop the couscous onto heated plates and garnish with the halloumi. Serve hot.

It's that easy: Be sure to stir the couscous into the hot liquid so that it softens and swells evenly.

Extra hungry? Stir in some of the leftover chickpeas from the can.

In the glass: We sampled Redgate Creek Reserve Selection Sauvignon Blanc with this dish and loved the bright citrus and mineral flavors.

Superfood Salad

There's a lot of talk about superfoods nowadays and how certain ingredients are packed with vitamins and minerals. This salad is my stab at throwing all the good stuff in one bowl and making dinner out of it. "Good for you" is a fine goal, but delicious . . . now that's what I'm talking about.

3 Tbsp olive oil	1 ripe mango, pitted, peeled, and diced
1 onion, diced	1/4 cup [30 g] slivered almonds
1/2 cup [90 g] quinoa, rinsed	2 Tbsp fresh lemon juice
1 cup [240 ml] vegetable broth	Kosher salt and freshly ground black pepper
2 cups [140 g] thinly sliced kale leaves	1/2 cup [60 g] crumbled feta cheese
1 cup [170 g] blueberries	

1. Heat a 12-in [30.5-cm] skillet over medium-high heat, and add 1 Tbsp of the olive oil. When the oil shimmers, add the onion and cook until it begins to soften, about 2 minutes. Add the quinoa and stir to coat the grains with the oil. Pour in the vegetable broth and bring to a simmer. Cover, turn the heat to low, and gently simmer until the quinoa is tender, about 20 minutes.

2. Add the kale and cook, tossing off of the heat, until it wilts in the hot grains, about 2 minutes. Transfer the quinoa mixture to a large bowl to cool slightly. After about 5 minutes, stir in the blueberries, mango, and almonds.

3. Meanwhile, in a medium bowl, whisk together the lemon juice, remaining 2 Tbsp olive oil, 1/4 tsp salt, and a few grinds of pepper. Pour the dressing over the quinoa mixture and toss to coat well. Taste and season with more salt and pepper, if it needs it. Gently fold in the feta.

4. Scoop the salad into bowls and serve warm or at room temperature.

continued

GRAINS & BEANS WITH SOUL

It's that easy: *It's almost as hard to find a ripe mango in the grocery store as it is to find a ripe avocado. Much like an avocado, a ripe mango's flesh yields to pressure. Mangoes also turn more golden when ripe. A mango pit is wide and flat, so the fruit can be tricky to dice. Look at the mango and notice that there are two flatter sides. Holding the stem end down, cut into the mango, slightly off center, starting from the pointed top and moving down one of the flat sides. Try to get as close to the pit as possible. Repeat on the other side. There will be a little flesh left adhering to the pit but you can nibble that yourself for a little snack.*

Extra hungry? *Grate a hard-boiled egg or two into the salad.*

In the glass: *Look for a bottle of Sauvignon Blanc from Frog's Leap.*

Barley Salad

with FENNEL and NECTARINE "PICO DE GALLO"

Barley is one of my favorite grains. I love its springy texture, and it cooks up fast, fast, fast. The sugar snap peas add crispness and color but what makes this salad special is the fennel and nectarine "pico de gallo" topping. Crunchy and juicy at the same time, this dish is really two salads in one. Prepping the vegetables while the barley cooks really speeds things up.

2 cups [480 ml] water	*Zest of 1 orange*
½ cup [100 g] pearled barley, rinsed	*Freshly ground black pepper*
Kosher salt	*2 nectarines, peeled and cut into bite-size pieces, juices reserved*
2 cups [180 g] sugar snap peas	
3 Tbsp white wine vinegar	*½ head fennel, cored and thinly sliced, plus a few fronds, minced*
½ tsp Dijon mustard	
1 shallot, finely diced	*Leaves from 3 or 4 sprigs basil, thinly sliced*
¼ cup [60 ml] extra-virgin olive oil	*1 head Treviso lettuce, thinly sliced*
2 Tbsp minced flat-leaf parsley	*2 oz [55 g] ricotta salata cheese, grated*

1. In a 3-qt [2.8-L] saucepan over medium-high heat, bring the water to a boil. Add the barley and ½ tsp salt and bring to a simmer. Turn the heat to low, cover, and gently simmer until the barley is tender, about 20 minutes. When the barley is tender, add the sugar snap peas and simmer until the peas are tender-crisp, about 3 minutes. Drain the barley and peas in a fine-mesh sieve and run cold water over them to cool slightly and stop the cooking. Set aside.

2. In a large bowl, whisk together the vinegar, mustard, shallot, and ¼ tsp salt until the salt dissolves. Whisk in the olive oil, parsley, orange zest, and a few grinds of pepper to form a vinaigrette.

3. Transfer 2 Tbsp of the vinaigrette to a small bowl. Add the nectarines and their juices, the fennel and fronds, and basil and toss to coat well. Set the "pico de gallo" aside.

continued

GRAINS & BEANS WITH SOUL

4. Add the barley mixture, Treviso, and ricotta salata to the large bowl of vinaigrette and toss to coat well. Taste and season with more salt and pepper, if it needs it.

5. Scoop the salad into bowls and top with the "pico de gallo." Serve immediately.

It's that easy: Ricotta salata is a firm Italian cheese with a mild, salty flavor. It's perfect in salads (like this one), grated over beets, tossed with escarole, or shaved onto roasted tomatoes.

Extra hungry? Add unseasoned purchased croutons to the salad and eat them fast—before they get soggy.

In the glass: Nobilo is my go-to Sauvignon Blanc at the moment because it can stand up to tart flavors, like the ones in the nectarines and the vinaigrette.

Farro Salad

with FENNEL, RADICCHIO, *and* PISTACHIOS

I love farro, and this salad is a wonderful combination of the chewy good-for-you grain with sweet orange, bitter radicchio, and crunchy fennel. There is nothing I'd rather eat on a hot summer's night. I would prefer to be sitting outside gazing at the sea, of course, but my backyard in Ohio will do in a pinch.

1½ cups [360 ml] water	*¼ cup [60 ml] olive oil*
Kosher salt	*¼ cup [30 g] chopped pistachios*
½ cup [90 g] farro, rinsed	*½ small head fennel, cored and thinly sliced*
1 garlic clove, smashed	*½ small head radicchio, cored and thinly sliced*
2 Tbsp rice vinegar	*2 oz [55 g] Manchego cheese, cut into small matchsticks*
Freshly ground black pepper	*2 Tbsp minced fresh flat-leaf parsley*
1 navel orange, zested, sectioned, and juice squeezed from center membranes and reserved	

1. In a 3-qt [2.8-L] saucepan over medium-high heat, bring the water to a boil. Add 1 tsp salt and the farro. Turn the heat to low, cover, and simmer until the farro is tender but still chewy, about 20 minutes. Drain in a fine-mesh sieve and run cold water over the farro to cool slightly and stop the cooking. Set aside.

2. Meanwhile, in a large bowl, stir together the garlic, vinegar, ¼ tsp salt, and a few grinds of pepper. Let sit until the garlic flavors the vinegar, about 5 minutes, then discard the garlic. Stir in the orange zest and orange juice, then whisk in the olive oil.

3. Add the pistachios, fennel, radicchio, orange sections, Manchego, parsley, and cooled farro (it's okay if it's still a little warm) and toss to coat well. Taste and season with more salt and pepper, if it needs it.

4. Scoop the salad into shallow bowls and serve at room temperature.

It's that easy: *I ask you to zest and section an orange in this recipe so this is how you do it. First, zest the orange with a Microplane and set the zest aside. Next, cut the peel from the two ends of the orange to reveal the flesh underneath. Set the orange on a cutting board, cut-side down, and cut away the peel and pith with a sharp knife, following the round shape. Flip the orange, check the underside, and cut away any white pith that remains. Now cut the orange sections between the membranes, dropping the sections and juices into a bowl as you work your way around the fruit. You will be left with a bowl of glistening orange crescents and a handful of orangey membrane. Squeeze the membrane of any remaining juice and reserve that for the dressing. Discard the membrane and proceed with the recipe.*

Extra hungry? *Toss in 1 cup [220 g] chickpeas (you may have leftovers from the Couscous with Broccolini, Chickpeas, and Fried Halloumi on page 108) for a punch of protein.*

In the glass: *Something white and light like a Pinot Blanc from Eyrie Vineyards in Oregon's Willamette Valley.*

Farro Primavera

It couldn't be simpler to pull this meatless dinner together. To save time, I like to cut up all the veggies and make the pesto while the farro cooks. It uses all the sweet root vegetables that chilly spring insists we polish off before taking up with more tender fare. Carrot, parsnip, celery root, and peas interspersed with nutty grains and coated in a basil-flecked sauce makes this springtime meal filling and delicious.

2 cups [480 ml] water

Kosher salt

¾ cup [135 g] farro, rinsed

1 carrot, cut into ½-in [12-mm] dice

1 parsnip, peeled and cut into ½-in [12-mm] dice

½ small celery root, peeled and cut into ½-in [12-mm] dice

1 Tbsp olive oil

1 shallot, diced

1 cup [140 g] grape tomatoes, halved

Freshly ground black pepper

¼ cup [60 ml] vegetable broth

2 Tbsp unsalted butter

½ cup [120 ml] basil pesto

½ cup [70 g] frozen peas, thawed

Red pepper flakes for seasoning (optional)

1. In a 3-qt [2.8-L] saucepan over medium-high heat, bring the water to a boil. Add 1 tsp salt and the farro and return the pot to a boil. Turn the heat to low and simmer until the farro is almost tender but still chewy, about 15 minutes. Add the carrot, parsnip, and celery root; turn the heat to medium-high; and cook until the farro and vegetables are tender, about 5 minutes longer. Drain the farro and vegetables in a fine-mesh sieve. Set aside.

2. Add the olive oil to the hot pan and set over medium-high heat. When the oil shimmers, add the shallot and cook until it softens, about 3 minutes. Add the tomatoes and cook until they're warmed through, about 1 minute. Add the farro mixture and season with salt and black pepper. Add the vegetable broth, butter, pesto, and peas and cook, tossing, until the peas are warmed through and the flavors blend, about 2 minutes. Taste and season with more salt, black pepper, or red pepper flakes, if it needs it.

3. Spoon the primavera into heated shallow bowls and serve hot.

It's that easy: Farro is a wheat-like grain, commonly confused with spelt. It fell out of favor hundreds of years ago when other, higher-yield grains were found to be easier to grow. But it's had a resurgence of popularity in the last ten years or so thanks to foodies like you and me. It has a firm bite and nutty texture kind of like wheat berries, though it takes less time to cook.

Extra hungry? Julienne a zucchini with one of those julienne peelers and toss it with a splash of lemon juice and olive oil and a sprinkle of salt and pepper.

In the glass: I'd love to splurge here with a Ridge Chardonnay as this dinner is certainly worth an expensive bottle. If that's too spendy, try Four Vines Santa Barbara County Naked Chardonnay for much less.

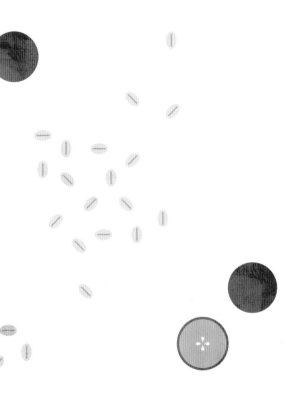

. . . .
START TO FINISH
30 minutes
. . .
HANDS-ON TIME
30 minutes
. . .
Serves 2
. . . .

Indonesian Fried Rice

There has never been a better use for leftover rice than nasi goreng, an Indonesian staple that usually includes ingredients like *kecap manis* (Indonesian sweet soy sauce) and tamarind, which can be hard to come by in Western grocery stores. To simplify this dish, I've taken some liberties with the ingredient list and come up with good substitutions, while keeping the full monty of spice, sweet-tart flavor, and vegetables.

2 Tbsp molasses

2 Tbsp soy sauce, plus more as needed

1 tsp chile-garlic sauce, sambal oelek, or Sriracha

¹/₂ tsp vegan fish sauce

2 eggs

1 tsp sesame oil

2 tsp vegetable oil

1 shallot, minced

2 garlic cloves, minced

One 2-in [5-cm] knob fresh ginger, peeled and minced

1 stalk lemongrass, white part only, thinly sliced

2 cups [120 g] thinly sliced cabbage

1 carrot, cut into matchsticks

¹/₂ tsp kosher salt

Freshly ground black pepper

3 cups [360 g] cold cooked white rice

2 Tbsp minced fresh cilantro

¹/₄ cucumber, peeled, seeded, and diced

1. In a small bowl, stir together the molasses, soy sauce, chile-garlic sauce, and fish sauce. In another small bowl, whisk together the eggs and sesame oil. Set aside.

2. Heat a 12-in [30.5-cm] skillet over medium-high heat, and add the vegetable oil. When the oil shimmers, add the shallot, garlic, ginger, and lemongrass and cook until fragrant and softened, about 1 minute. Add the cabbage, carrot, salt, and a few grinds of pepper and cook until the vegetables are tender, about 4 minutes.

3. Add the rice and the molasses mixture and stir to combine with the vegetables until the rice is hot, about 4 minutes. Drizzle the egg mixture over the hot rice and vegetables and cook, tossing and stirring, until the eggs are set, about 2 minutes longer. Taste and season with more soy sauce or pepper, if it needs it.

4. Scoop the rice into heated shallow bowls, sprinkle with the cilantro, and serve with the diced cucumber.

It's that easy: *You can find the chile-garlic sauce and fish sauce in the international aisle of many grocery stores these days. They last for a long time in the refrigerator. You'll discover that the chile-garlic sauce is wonderful in soups and stews, and the fish sauce adds a savory edge to dipping sauces and even chicken soup.*

Extra hungry? *Add an additional 1 cup [110 g] cabbage and ½ cup [60 g] rice.*

In the glass: *A Spanish Rioja has the fruit and spice to stand up to the strong flavors of this dish. One widely available bottle and a great buy for the money is Marqués de Cáceres Crianza.*

Butternut Risotto

Local butternut squash is tasty and plentiful where I live. I usually buy them from a little unmanned stand just outside of town, where I leave my dollar in a lockbox and walk away with a prime specimen. Every time I cut one open, the flesh drips with sweet juice. You'll use just the neck of a medium squash for this recipe. For another meal, go ahead and bake off the remaining hollowed end with butter and maple syrup in a low oven. Now that, I could eat for dessert.

2 Tbsp unsalted butter

1 onion, diced

The neck of a medium butternut squash, about 1 lb [455 g], peeled and cut into 1/2-in [12-mm] dice

1 cup [200 g] Arborio rice

Kosher salt

1/3 cup [80 ml] white wine

3 cups [720 ml] warm vegetable broth, plus more as needed

1 lemon, zested and cut in half

1/2 cup [15 g] grated Parmesan cheese, plus shaved Parmesan for garnish

Freshly ground black pepper

1/4 cup [60 ml] heavy cream (optional)

1 Tbsp minced fresh flat-leaf parsley

1. Heat a 12-in [30.5-cm] skillet over medium heat, and melt the butter. When the butter sizzles, add the onion and squash, toss it in the fat, and cook until the vegetables begin to soften, about 3 minutes. Add the rice and 1/2 tsp salt and sauté, stirring until the rice is opaque and smells toasty, about 4 minutes. Add the wine (it will bubble up) and cook until the liquid evaporates and the pan is almost dry, about 1 minute.

2. Add about 1/2 cup [120 ml] of the vegetable broth to the pan and cook, stirring every now and then as the rice begins to look creamy. Turn the heat to medium-low. Now, in spite of what you may have heard, you don't have to stand there and be a slave to your risotto. Just give it a stir every few minutes to keep it from sticking to the pan. When the broth is absorbed and the risotto starts to look dry, add another 1/2 cup [120 ml] broth and cook, stirring occasionally, until absorbed. Keep adding the broth in 1/2-cup [120-ml] increments, stirring every now and then. Turn the heat to low if it's bubbling too much. You want the risotto to simmer slowly.

3. After about 10 minutes of cooking, add the lemon zest and cook, adding more broth as necessary, until the rice and squash are tender, about 15 minutes longer. (If you run out of broth, just add hot water.) When the rice is al dente and the squash is tender, stir in the grated Parmesan. Taste and season with salt and pepper, if it needs it. I can't resist adding the heavy cream, but you decide if you need that luxurious boost or not. Give the risotto a little squeeze of juice from the lemon halves. I usually add the juice from a cut lemon half and then add a touch more on top of that. If the risotto is too thick, stir in a bit more broth or hot water. (I like my risotto a little bit on the liquidy side. Once again, it's your choice.)

4. Spoon the risotto into heated shallow bowls and garnish with the parsley and shaved Parmesan. Slurp happily.

It's that easy: Be sure to cut the squash into little dice. That way they will have time to become tender and become one with the risotto.

Extra hungry? If you or your significant other needs a little more to make this a meal, just toss up a salad of Boston lettuce, grape tomatoes, and chives. Lightly dress with a splash of white wine vinegar and a glug of olive oil. It's one of my favorite ways to bulk up dinner when I'm not so hungry, but my husband is famished.

In the glass: Look for wines with hints of grapefruit and grass in them such as Kim Crawford Sauvignon Blanc. And don't forget to chill it a little more than you would a Chardonnay.

Red Quinoa Risotto

with ASPARAGUS *and* PARMESAN

Risotto is my jam. Whether made with Arborio rice, barley, or quinoa, I love the feel of hot chewy grains sliding into my belly. The spring and nutty texture of the red quinoa is a nice change of pace from the usual rice-based risottos, but you do have to add a little cream to make it creamy—not necessarily a bad thing.

1 Tbsp olive oil

1 Tbsp unsalted butter

1 onion, diced

1 garlic clove, minced

Kosher salt

1 cup [170 g] red quinoa, rinsed

½ cup [120 ml] white wine

2 cups [480 ml] vegetable broth, plus more as needed

12 stalks asparagus, trimmed and cut into 1-in [2.5-cm] pieces, tips reserved

⅓ cup [80 ml] heavy cream, plus more as needed

⅓ cup [10 g] grated Parmesan cheese

Freshly ground black pepper

1 Tbsp minced fresh flat-leaf parsley

1. Heat a 12-in [30.5-cm] skillet over medium-high heat, and add the olive oil and butter. When the butter melts and sizzles, add the onion, garlic, and ½ tsp salt and cook until the onion begins to soften, about 2 minutes. Add the quinoa and stir to coat the grains with the fat. Add the wine (it will bubble up) and cook until the liquid evaporates and the pan is almost dry, about 1 minute.

2. Add the vegetable broth and bring to a simmer. Turn the heat to low, cover, and simmer until the quinoa is almost tender, about 15 minutes. Add the asparagus stalks and cook, uncovered, for 3 minutes, then add the asparagus tips and cook until the

tips and quinoa are tender, about 2 minutes. Stir in the cream. If the risotto is a little soupy, cook until the liquid evaporates, a few minutes longer. If it's a little dry, add more broth or cream. Bring to a simmer again and stir in about half of the Parmesan. Taste and season with more salt and pepper, if it needs it.

3. Spoon the risotto into heated bowls and sprinkle with the remaining Parmesan and the parsley. Serve hot.

It's that easy: *Red quinoa is, well, red. It cooks in about the same time as white quinoa, though the grains of red and black quinoa when cooked tend to be more distinct and less mushy than the white variety. Feel free to use red, black, or white quinoa in this recipe.*

Extra hungry? *How about garlic bread? Drizzle country-style bread with olive oil and toast it in the toaster. Rub with a peeled clove of raw garlic while the toast is still hot.*

In the glass: *There's something about a fizzy white wine with a dish that's as creamy and decadent as this one. Look for a bottle of Nepenthe sparkling Sauvignon Blanc for bubbles and bright acidity.*

START TO FINISH
40 minutes
...
HANDS-ON TIME
20 minutes
...
Serves 2

Fried Quinoa

with KALE and KIMCHI

Kale and kimchi unite! This dish has a decidedly Korean flavor, with ingredients like gochujang and kimchi, both of which are fermented and good for you. I could go on about the healthfulness of this dish, with the kale and quinoa and all, but I'd much rather tell you how delicious it is. Make this tonight; it's delish.

2 Tbsp vegetable oil	*2 tsp gochujang*
1 onion, diced	*1 Tbsp soy sauce, plus more as needed*
1 garlic clove, minced	*1 tsp sesame oil*
1 bunch kale, ribs removed, chopped	*2 eggs*
Kosher salt	*³/₄ cup [150 g] kimchi, chopped, plus more as needed*
1 cup [170 g] quinoa, rinsed	*1 green onion, white and green parts, thinly sliced*
2 cups [480 ml] vegetable broth	

1. Heat a 12-in [30.5-cm] skillet over medium-high heat, and add the vegetable oil. When the oil shimmers, add the onion and sauté until it begins to soften, about 2 minutes. Add the garlic, kale, and ¹/₄ tsp salt and sauté until the kale softens and turns bright green, about 2 minutes longer. Add the quinoa and vegetable broth and bring to a simmer. Cover, turn the heat to low, and simmer for 10 minutes. Turn off the heat and let sit, covered, for another 10 minutes, until the quinoa absorbs the remaining liquid. Uncover and if there is still some liquid in the skillet, cook over medium-high heat, stirring, until it evaporates, about 1 minute.

2. In a small bowl, stir together the gochujang, soy sauce, and sesame oil. In another small bowl, beat together the eggs and ¹/₄ tsp salt.

3. Return the quinoa to medium-high heat and add the gochujang mixture and kimchi, stirring, until warmed through, about 1 minute. Pour in the eggs and cook, stirring and scraping up anything that may be stuck on the bottom of the pan, until the eggs cook into small clumps, about 1 minute. Taste and add more soy sauce if you'd like more saltiness or more kimchi if you'd like more heat and acidity.

continued

GRAINS & BEANS WITH SOUL

127

4. Spoon the quinoa into heated bowls and garnish with the green onion. Serve hot.

It's that easy: Both sweet and spicy, gochujang is a Korean chile sauce that's made from chiles, rice, fermented soybeans, and salt. You can buy it in small tubs at Asian markets and some grocery stores. It will keep for months and months in the refrigerator, and you can use it like you would a barbecue sauce on just about anything you'd like to spice up. Kimchi is a spicy condiment of (usually) pickled cabbage and peppers. Both spicy and tart, it adds interest to soups, stews, egg dishes, and wraps. It can be a little stinky, I'm not gonna lie, but you don't have to smell it. Just eat it; it's so good.

Extra hungry? Add another egg to make the dish more substantial.

In the glass: A Riesling from Trimbach is easy to find and easy on the wallet. Rieslings are famous for matching up with spicy Asian flavors because they are dry but with a softly sweet edge that mellows Asian food's spicy side.

Moroccan Freekeh

with BUTTERNUT SQUASH *and* KOHLRABI

Commonly found in North Africa and the Middle East, freekeh is a young, green wheat that has been lightly toasted, creating a smoky, nutty texture that's similar to bulgur. Higher in protein and lower on the glycemic index than many grains, it's not only tasty but good for you as well. The kohlrabi, raisins, and butternut squash add sweetness, the almonds extra crunch, and the spices will waft you away to a souk in the Casbah.

2 Tbsp olive oil, plus more for drizzling

1 leek, white part only, cleaned and sliced

½ tsp ground cumin

½ tsp ground cinnamon

½ tsp ras el hanout or other Moroccan spice blend

1 cup [150 g] cracked freekeh

2 cups [480 ml] vegetable broth

2 cups [230 g] diced butternut squash

2 cups [230 g] diced kohlrabi

¼ cup [40 g] raisins

¼ cup [30 g] slivered almonds

¼ cup [7 g] chopped flat-leaf parsley

Zest and juice of ½ lemon, plus more juice as needed

Kosher salt and freshly ground black pepper

1. Heat a 12-in [30.5-cm] skillet over medium-high heat, and add the olive oil. When the oil shimmers, add the leek and cook until it begins to soften, about 1 minute. Add the cumin, cinnamon, ras el hanout, and freekeh and cook, stirring, until the grain is lightly toasted, about 1 minute. Add the vegetable broth, butternut squash, kohlrabi, and raisins and bring to a simmer. Turn the heat to low, cover, and simmer until the freekeh and vegetables are tender, about 20 minutes. Turn off the heat.

continued

2. Stir the almonds, parsley, lemon zest, and lemon juice into the pan and drizzle with more olive oil. Taste and season with salt, pepper, and more lemon juice, if it needs it.

3. Spoon the freekeh into shallow bowls. Serve hot or at room temperature.

It's that easy: *Every brand of North African ras el hanout will contain a different blend of spices. Most common are cardamom, clove, cinnamon, ground chile, coriander, cumin, peppercorn, paprika, fenugreek, and turmeric. If you can't find ras el hanout, just add a mix of some of these spices that you may have in your spice drawer. It will be delicious.*

Extra hungry? *Serve with pita bread and hummus.*

In the glass: *Something light and fruity like an Italian Pinot Grigio would work well alongside this hearty dish. Look for Kris or Cavit Pinot Grigio from the Veneto in Northeastern Italy.*

Dal Makhani

with CRISPY LEEK

Lentils, beans, and split peas (all legumes) are referred to as *dal* in Indian cuisine. Legumes are really the backbone of Indian meals and supply much-needed protein to what is often a vegetarian diet. The spices and aromatics in this dal elevate the simple lentil to another level of delicious. I like to make this dal thick and serve it as a dip with bread, but you can also thin it out and serve over rice for more substantial appetites.

3 Tbsp unsalted butter

1 leek, white part only, cleaned and thinly sliced

1 small onion, chopped

2 garlic cloves, minced

One 2-in [5-cm] knob fresh ginger, peeled and minced

1 Tbsp tomato paste

1 tsp garam masala

¼ tsp turmeric

Pinch of ground clove

Pinch of cayenne pepper

Kosher salt and freshly ground black pepper

1 cup [180 g] black, red, or brown lentils, sorted and rinsed

2½ cups [600 ml] vegetable broth, plus more as needed

1 Tbsp fresh lemon juice, plus more as needed

1 Tbsp minced fresh cilantro

Chapati or naan for serving

1. Heat a 12-in [30.5-cm] skillet over medium-high heat, and melt 2 Tbsp of the butter. When the butter sizzles, add the leek and sauté until browned, 6 to 8 minutes. Transfer the leek to a plate and set aside.

2. Add the remaining 1 Tbsp butter, the onion, garlic, and ginger to the hot pan and cook until the onion begins to soften, about 3 minutes. Add the tomato paste, garam masala, turmeric, clove, cayenne, ½ tsp salt, and a few grinds of black pepper

and cook, stirring, until the spices are fragrant and the vegetables soften, about 2 minutes longer.

3. Add the lentils and vegetable broth and bring to a simmer. Turn the heat to low, cover, and simmer until the lentils are tender, 20 to 25 minutes. Turn off the heat and stir in the lemon juice and, with a potato masher, smash the lentils until a rough purée forms. Taste and season with more salt, black pepper, or lemon juice, if it needs it. For a thinner texture, stir in more broth.

4. Spoon the dal onto heated plates and scatter the cilantro and leek over the top. Serve with the chapati on the side for scooping.

It's that easy: *Cooking times for lentils will vary according to how fresh they are. Do a taste test after the suggested cooking times and if they need a few extra minutes of cooking and a little more liquid, give it to them. The cooked lentils should be soft and yielding with no crunchy centers.*

Extra hungry? *How about some fruit. Slice up a mango or a few strawberries to serve on the side.*

In the glass: *Something earthy, juicy, and red, like a Bodega Catena Zapata Malbec.*

Spiced Green Lentils

with SWEET POTATO and PISTACHIOS

These pretty green lentils are often called *lentilles du Puy*, or French lentils. They cook pretty much the same way as everyday brown lentils and even the more exotic black beluga lentils, so you can substitute with any variety you like. I love how this dish fills me up and how the sweet potato is like a little dessert in the middle of dinner.

---

2 Tbsp olive oil, plus more for drizzling

1 tsp coriander seeds, coarsely ground in a mortar and pestle

1 tsp cumin seeds, coarsely ground in a mortar and pestle

Pinch of ground clove

1 onion, chopped

1 garlic clove, minced

1 sweet potato, peeled and cut into ¹/₂-in [12-mm] chunks

Kosher salt and freshly ground black pepper

³/₄ cup [135 g] green lentils, sorted and rinsed

1³/₄ cups [420 ml] vegetable broth, plus more as needed

¹/₂ lemon

¹/₄ cup [30 g] pistachios, coarsely chopped

2 oz [55 g] goat cheese, crumbled

¹/₃ cup [60 g] pomegranate seeds

1 Tbsp chopped fresh flat-leaf parsley

1 Tbsp chopped fresh mint

---

1. Heat a 12-in [30.5-cm] skillet over medium-high heat, and add the olive oil. When the oil shimmers, add the coriander, cumin, clove, onion, garlic, sweet potato, ¹/₄ tsp salt, and a few grinds of pepper and sauté until the onion begins to soften and the garlic is fragrant, about 3 minutes. Add the lentils and vegetable broth and bring to a simmer. Turn the heat to low, cover, and simmer until the lentils and vegetables are tender and the liquid has been absorbed, about 30 minutes. (Check after 15 minutes to see if the lentils need a little more broth to cover.) Turn off the heat.

2. Squeeze the lemon over the lentils and stir in the pistachios. Taste and season with more salt and pepper, if it needs it.

3. Scoop the lentils into heated bowls and sprinkle with the goat cheese, pomegranate seeds, parsley, and mint. Serve hot or at room temperature.

It's that easy: *Pistachios are always in my pantry. Salty and buttery, they add oomph to salads and are a tasty snack to eat straight from the bag. Buy them; you'll be glad to have them on hand.*

Extra hungry? *Tear up some escarole leaves and toss with the juice from the leftover half of lemon. Add a glug of olive oil and a few halved grape tomatoes.*

In the glass: *A light and fruity Pinot Noir or Chardonnay from A to Z is my choice. Don't let the screw cap fool you. This is a great bottle for the money.*

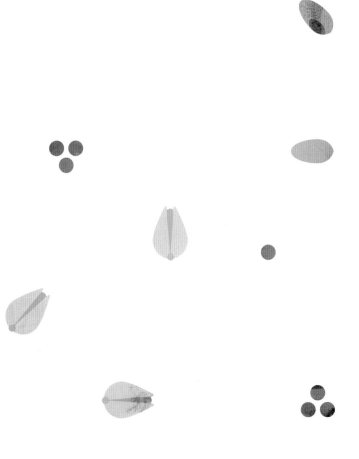

135

Falafel

Falafel can often disappoint in a restaurant (much like crab cakes), but did you know that these crispy nuggets are especially delicious when you make them at home? All you have to do is blend up some canned chickpeas with other flavorful things, fry them up quickly, tuck them into pita bread, and eat them immediately. Now that I can do.

One 15-oz [425-g] can chickpeas, drained

1 garlic clove, minced

1/2 small onion, finely diced

1 egg, beaten

2 Tbsp chopped fresh flat-leaf parsley

2 Tbsp all-purpose flour

2 tsp fresh lemon juice

1/2 tsp ground cumin

1/2 tsp ground coriander

Pinch of cayenne pepper

Kosher salt and freshly ground black pepper

1/2 cup [120 ml] vegetable oil

2 pita breads

Sliced tomatoes, lettuce or spinach leaves, pickled peppers, thinly sliced red onion, and thinly sliced cucumbers for serving

Purchased tahini sauce for drizzling

1. In a medium bowl, mash the chickpeas with a potato masher until broken up but still a little chunky. Add the garlic, onion, and egg and stir until combined, then add the parsley and flour and stir until combined (the chickpeas will continue to break down). Add the lemon juice, cumin, coriander, cayenne, 1/2 tsp salt, and a few grinds of black pepper and stir until well combined.

2. With an ice-cream scoop or spoon, scoop the chickpea mixture into eight golf ball–size rounds (I like to use a trigger ice cream scoop). Place the falafel rounds on a plate and refrigerate, uncovered, for about 15 minutes.

continued

3. Heat a 12-in [30.5-cm] skillet over medium-high heat, and add the vegetable oil. When the oil shimmers, pinch off a piece of falafel from one of the balls and slide it into the oil. If it sizzles and browns, the oil is ready. With a spatula, gently flatten the balls (they'll be easier to brown on both sides) and slide them into the hot oil. Cook until browned on the bottom, about 2 minutes, then flip them with a fork or spatula to cook the second side until browned, about 2 minutes longer. Transfer the falafel rounds to a paper towel–lined plate and let cool for a few minutes while you assemble the pita.

4. Cut the pita rounds in half, split them open to make a pocket, and stuff them with some tomatoes, lettuce, pickled peppers, onion, and cucumbers to your taste. Tuck two falafel patties into each pita half and drizzle with tahini sauce. Serve hot.

It's that easy: Canned chickpeas can vary in texture and water content, so if your falafel mixture is too loose, add more flour, 1 Tbsp at a time, until the falafel balls hold together.

Extra hungry? Concoct a little salad of cucumber, arugula, lemon juice, and a glug of extra-virgin olive oil.

In the glass: I love an Albariño from Spain. Refreshing and light, this white wine is best served really cold.

Crunchy Black Bean Tacos

with CORN and QUESO FRESCO

Luckily for us, canned black beans are not only delicious, but they're easy to incorporate into busy weeknight meals. With their high protein content and big flavor, they satisfy vegetarians and omnivores alike. Crisping up the tortillas adds another texture and warms up these tacos, melting the cheese and creating a cross between a taco and a quesadilla. Call them what you will; I call them delish.

4 Tbsp [60 g] olive oil

1 small onion, chopped

½ tsp ground cumin

One 15-oz [425-g] can seasoned black beans, drained and rinsed

¾ cup [105 g] fresh or thawed frozen corn

2 Tbsp minced fresh cilantro

Juice from ½ lime

Kosher salt and freshly ground black pepper

Eight 6-in [15-cm] corn tortillas

4 oz [115 g] crumbled queso fresco or other farmer cheese

Diced avocado, jarred salsa, pickled jalapeños, and sour cream for serving

1. Heat a 12-in [30.5-cm] skillet over medium-high heat, and add 1 Tbsp of the olive oil. When the oil shimmers, add the onion and cumin and sauté until the onion begins to soften, about 3 minutes. Transfer the onion to a medium bowl. Add the black beans, corn, cilantro, lime juice, ½ tsp salt, and a few grinds of pepper to the onion and mash lightly with the back of a fork.

2. Add 1 Tbsp olive oil to the hot skillet and set over medium-high heat. Working in batches, place two tortillas in the pan. Fill one half of each tortilla with about ¼ cup [50 g] of the black bean mixture and

sprinkle with the cheese. Carefully fold over the empty half of the tortilla to enclose the filling, and cook until the bottom is crispy, about 3 minutes.

3. With a spatula, carefully flip the tacos and cook the second side until crispy and the filling is warmed through, about 3 minutes. Turn the heat to medium if the tacos begin to burn; you want to be sure the filling warms up. Transfer the tacos to a low oven to keep warm and repeat with the remaining olive oil, tortillas, and filling.

continued

4. Arrange the tacos on heated plates and serve with avocado, salsa, jalapeños, and sour cream on the side.

It's that easy: Corn tortillas are ever so much tastier when crisped up in some oil. Make these good and crispy, and don't worry if some of the filling escapes when you flip them. The filling will brown and become even more tasty when you stuff it back inside.

Extra hungry? Dice up some of the avocado and blend it in ½ cup [115 g] or so of the salsa. Add some salty tortilla chips for dipping.

In the glass: A nicely chilled rosé like Muga Rioja Rosado or an ice-cold Dos Equis—it's your call.

Black Beans

with BARLEY, SWEET POTATO, *and* CHIPOTLE

A sweet potato adds just the right amount of starch, color, and sweetness to this simple week-night meal. The chewy barley replaces the meat, while the chipotle adds the heat. I like to call this kind of recipe a pantry staple since so many of the ingredients can be found in your cupboards, just waiting for their cue to appear on the dinner table.

---

1 Tbsp olive oil

1 small onion, diced

1 garlic clove, minced

1 Tbsp chili powder

1 tsp coriander seeds, coarsely ground in a mortar and pestle

1 tsp dried oregano

Kosher salt and freshly ground black pepper

One 15-oz [425-g] can seasoned black beans, drained and rinsed

One 14¹/₂-oz [411-g] can fire-roasted diced tomatoes or plain diced tomatoes with juice

¹/₂ canned chipotle chile in adobo, finely chopped

1 sweet potato, peeled and diced

¹/₃ cup [60 g] pearled barley, rinsed

1¹/₂ cups [360 ml] vegetable broth, plus more as needed

2 Tbsp fresh minced cilantro

Queso fresco, sour cream, or yogurt for serving

---

1. Heat a 12-in [30.5-cm] skillet over medium-high heat, and add the olive oil. When the oil shimmers, add the onion, garlic, chili powder, coriander, oregano, ¹/₄ tsp salt, and a few grinds of pepper. Sauté until the onion begins to soften, about 3 minutes.

2. Add the black beans, tomatoes, chipotle, sweet potato, barley, and vegetable broth to the pan and bring to a simmer. Push the sweet potato to submerge it in the liquid, then turn the heat to low, cover, and simmer until the barley and sweet potato are tender, about 20 minutes. Taste and season with more salt and pepper, if it needs it. If the consistency is too soupy, cook, uncovered, until the liquid is reduced and flavor concentrates, a few minutes longer. If it's a little dry, add more broth, ¹/₄ cup [60 ml] at a time, until it looks right. Turn off the heat and stir in 1 Tbsp of the cilantro.

3. Scoop the beans into heated bowls. Sprinkle with the remaining 1 Tbsp cilantro and top with queso fresco. Serve hot.

It's that easy: *Canned chipotle chiles come packed in a spicy tomatoey adobo sauce that enhances the flavor of the chiles, so don't scrape it all off. These chiles are hot, so if you're sensitive to the heat, add a little at a time until it tastes just right. There are more chiles than you can use at once packed in that little can, so freeze the rest, flat, in a plastic bag to use another time. Look for seasoned black beans on your grocery shelf as they have a little more flavor than unseasoned.*

Extra hungry? *You can always serve this with cornbread from the grocery store's bakery department. Mine sells it by the quarter round, which is the perfect amount for two.*

In the glass: *Spicy black beans and beer are a perfect match. My beer of choice here is Corona Light with a wedge of lime, but Top Hat, with its citrusy notes, would pair well too.*

Tuscan White Bean Salad

with SWEET POTATO and LEMON VINAIGRETTE

Crunchy romaine, creamy white beans, roasted sweet potato, salty Parmesan, and tart dressing—all tossed together in a little more than 30 minutes—makes this dinner hit all the right notes no matter what the season. If you've made a few dishes from this chapter already, I know you're loving the ease of pulling out a can of beans and dressing them up with some fresh vegetables. Dinner has never been so easy and light, yet filling.

1 medium sweet potato, peeled and cut into ¹/₂-in [12-mm] dice

4 Tbsp [60 ml] extra-virgin olive oil, plus more as needed

Kosher salt and freshly ground black pepper

2 Tbsp white balsamic vinegar

1 Tbsp fresh lemon juice

1 shallot, minced

1 tsp Dijon mustard

One 15-oz [425-g] can cannellini beans, drained and rinsed

2 cups [20 g] torn baby romaine lettuce

2 oz [55 g] Parmesan cheese, shaved with a vegetable peeler

3 Tbsp minced fresh flat-leaf parsley

1. Preheat the oven to 400°F [200°C]. Line a sheet pan with parchment paper.

2. Toss together the sweet potato, 1 Tbsp of the olive oil, a pinch of salt, and a few grinds of pepper. Spread the sweet potato on the prepared sheet pan. Roast until tender and lightly browned, about 25 minutes.

3. Meanwhile, in a large bowl, whisk together the vinegar, lemon juice, shallot, mustard, ¹/₄ tsp salt, and a few grinds of pepper and let sit until the flavors blend, about 5 minutes. Pour the remaining 3 Tbsp olive oil into the vinegar mixture in a thin stream, constantly whisking until an emulsion forms. Taste and season with more salt, pepper, or olive oil, if it needs it.

4. Add the cannellini beans, romaine, sweet potato, Parmesan, and parsley to the bowl and toss to coat with the dressing.

5. Mound the salad onto dinner plates or shallow bowls and serve immediately.

It's that easy: *Lining the sheet pan with parchment paper could mean no pan to wash, which is always a good thing.*

Extra hungry? *Lightly brush a few slices of bread with olive oil and toast them in the toaster. Rub with a clove of garlic while still hot and serve on the side. You can also roast a bigger sweet potato.*

In the glass: *Try a Sauvignon Blanc from Oyster Bay. If you're in the mood for red, a light Beaujolais would work as well.*

Pasta
for Dinner

....
START TO FINISH
15 minutes
...
HANDS-ON TIME
15 minutes
...
Serves 2
....

Spaghetti Cacio e Pepe

This simplest of pasta dishes requires the best of ingredients, so use a nice imported pasta, good cheese, and plenty of freshly ground black pepper. You'll be blown away by the flavor, texture, and simplicity of this Italian classic.

Kosher salt	*¹/₄ tsp red pepper flakes, plus more as needed*
8 oz [230 g] thin spaghetti, broken in half	*Freshly ground black pepper*
¹/₂ cup [30 g] grated pecorino romano cheese, plus more as needed	*1 Tbsp minced fresh flat-leaf parsley*

1. In a 3-qt [2.8-L] saucepan over high heat, bring 2 qt [2 L] water to a boil. Add 1 tsp salt and the spaghetti and cook until al dente (usually a minute or so less than the package directions). To check for doneness, fish out a strand and bite into it. It should still be chewy, just a little underdone.

2. Reserve ¹/₂ cup [120 ml] of the cooking water and then drain the pasta in a colander in the sink.

3. Return the pasta to the hot pan and pour in about ¹/₄ cup [60 ml] of the pasta water, the pecorino, red pepper flakes, and ¹/₄ tsp black pepper. Stir until a creamy sauce forms. If the pasta is dry, add more of the pasta water; if the sauce is a little too liquidy, add more cheese. Taste and season with more salt, black pepper, or red pepper flakes, if it needs it.

4. Mound the pasta onto heated plates and sprinkle with the parsley. Serve hot.

It's that easy: Resist the urge to buy cheese that's already grated. You can never be sure of the quality or if fillers have been added. Besides, everything always tastes best fresh, right? To speed things up, I like to break long spaghetti in half so that it's all submerged under-water when I put it in the pot.

Extra hungry? Keep it simple. Add a little salad of sliced tomatoes, arugula, a splash of red wine vinegar, a glug of olive oil, and salt and pepper to go with this classic dish.

In the glass: A red wine is definitely in order. Stick with an Italian theme and drink a glass of Ruffino Il Ducale, a blend of Sangiovese, Cabernet, and Merlot.

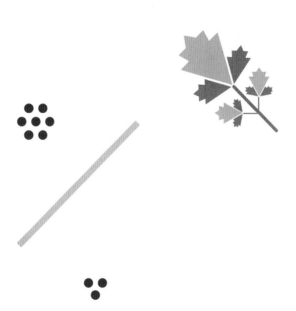

....
START TO FINISH
25 minutes
...
HANDS-ON TIME
25 minutes
...
Serves 2
....

Linguine

with RICOTTA, ZUCCHINI, SUN-DRIED TOMATO, *and* LEMON

Just like Norma Desmond, ricotta cheese is waiting for its close-up. After all, it's creamy, rich, and delicious just the way it is. All you have to do is toss it with hot pasta and punchy sun-dried tomatoes and you have a vegetarian noodle dish to rival pasta carbonara. Why didn't we think of this sooner? Prep the ingredients while the pasta is cooking, and this dish becomes one of the speediest in the book.

Kosher salt

8 oz [230 g] linguine, broken in half

1 Tbsp unsalted butter

One 6-in [15-cm] zucchini, quartered lengthwise and thinly sliced

2 garlic cloves, minced

¼ cup [40 g] chopped oil-packed sun-dried tomatoes, drained

¼ cup [40 g] frozen peas, thawed

½ cup [120 g] ricotta cheese

¼ cup [8 g] grated Parmesan cheese, plus more for sprinkling

Zest of 1 lemon, plus 2 Tbsp lemon juice

2 Tbsp chopped fresh flat-leaf parsley

Freshly ground black pepper

1. In a 3-qt [2.8-L] saucepan over high heat, bring 2 qt [2 L] water to a boil. Add 1 tsp salt and the linguine and cook until al dente (usually a minute or so less than the package directions). To check for doneness, fish out a strand and bite into it. It should still be chewy, just a little underdone.

2. Reserve ¼ cup [60 ml] of the cooking water and then drain the pasta in a colander in the sink. Run a little cold water (just a splash!) over the pasta to keep it from sticking together but don't cool it off too much.

3. Return the hot pan to high heat and add the butter, zucchini, garlic, and sun-dried tomatoes. Cook until the zucchini softens, about 4 minutes. Add the reserved cooking water, the peas, ricotta, Parmesan, lemon zest, lemon juice, parsley, and a few grinds of pepper and cook, stirring, until the sauce is hot, a minute or so.

4. Return the pasta to the pan and toss to reheat and coat with the sauce for another minute or so.

5. Mound the pasta into heated shallow bowls and sprinkle with more Parmesan. Serve hot.

It's that easy: *For some reason, most packages of dried pasta direct you to cook the pasta too long, especially if you're going to cook the pasta for a minute or so in the sauce. So if the package says to cook it for 11 minutes, check it at 9 minutes and again at the 10-minute mark. You want it to be firm but not crunchy, chewy but not hard . . . al dente.*

Extra hungry? *I don't know how you could still be hungry, but a fresh salad of thinly sliced radicchio dressed with a squeeze of lemon and a glug of olive oil would be a nice counterpoint to the rich pasta.*

In the glass: *This is a rich, cheesy pasta dish with some acidity in the tomatoes and lemon, so I'd go for an unoaked Chardonnay from Joel Gott. It's one of my favorites.*

Fresh Fettuccine

with WILD MUSHROOMS, GOAT CHEESE, and CHIVES

Fresh pasta is the ticket to the fastest and freshest dinners. These days, it's easy to find an assortment of fresh pasta in various flavors and shapes at most grocery stores. Which brings us to this super-simple classic of wild mushrooms and tangy goat cheese. Couldn't be easier. Couldn't be tastier.

Kosher salt

8 oz [230 g] fresh fettuccine

1 Tbsp unsalted butter

1 shallot, minced

1 garlic clove, minced

4 oz [115 g] fresh assorted wild or cremini mushrooms, thinly sliced

¼ cup [60 ml] dry white wine

⅓ cup [80 ml] heavy cream

2 oz [55 g] goat cheese, crumbled

Freshly ground black pepper

1 Tbsp fresh minced chives

1. In a 3-qt [2.8-L] saucepan over high heat, bring 2 qt [2 L] water to a boil. Add 1 tsp salt and the fettuccine and cook until al dente (usually a minute or so less than the package directions). To check for doneness, fish out a strand and bite into it. It should still be chewy, just a little underdone.

2. Reserve ½ cup [120 ml] of the cooking water and then drain the pasta in a colander in the sink. Run a little cold water (just a splash!) over the pasta to keep it from sticking together but don't cool it off too much.

3. Return the hot pan to medium-high heat and add the butter, shallot, garlic, mushrooms, and a pinch of salt. Cook until the mushrooms begin to soften, about 3 minutes. Add the wine and cook until the liquid is reduced by half, about 1 minute. Add the cream and goat cheese and cook, stirring, until the cheese melts and a creamy sauce forms, about 1 minute. Taste and season with a few grinds of pepper and more salt, if it needs it.

4. Return the pasta to the pan, pour in about ¼ cup [60 ml] of the pasta water, and toss to reheat the pasta and coat it well with the sauce. If the sauce is too sticky, add more of the pasta water.

5. Mound the pasta onto heated plates and sprinkle with the chives. Serve hot.

It's that easy: Be picky about your pasta. If there is a locally made product in your grocer's refrigerator case, buy it. The quality of locally made pasta will almost always be superior to the national brands.

Extra hungry? Add some thawed frozen bright green peas to the sauce.

In the glass: Crémant d'Alsace is a fizzy white wine from France that I love with this dish. You'll love the little bubbles and how they lighten the sturdy pasta and rich sauce.

Bow Ties

with BRUSSELS SPROUTS, GORGONZOLA, *and* HAZELNUTS

I've been making one version or another of this pasta for the last fifteen years. It's one of those quick-and-easy dishes that's still really impressive. When tossed with hot pasta, the Gorgonzola turns into an instant creamy sauce with chunks of Brussels sprouts and crunchy hazelnuts all cooked in one pan. Oh, yeah.

Kosher salt	*2 Tbsp unsalted butter*
8 oz [230 g] bow tie pasta	*1/3 cup [40 g] toasted and chopped hazelnuts*
15 Brussels sprouts, quartered	*2 Tbsp minced flat-leaf parsley*
4 oz [115 g] Gorgonzola cheese, crumbled	*Freshly ground black pepper (optional)*

1. In a 3-qt [2.8-L] saucepan over high heat, bring 2 qt [2 L] water to a boil. Add 1 tsp salt and the pasta and cook about 7 minutes. Add the Brussels sprouts and cook until the pasta is al dente and the Brussels sprouts are tender-crisp, 4 to 5 minutes longer. To check the pasta for doneness, fish out a bow tie and bite into it. It should still be chewy, just a little underdone.

2. Reserve 1/2 cup [120 ml] of the cooking water and then drain the pasta and Brussels sprouts in a colander in the sink.

3. Return the pasta and Brussels sprouts to the hot pan and pour in about 1/4 cup [60 ml] of the pasta water, the Gorgonzola, butter, hazelnuts, 1 Tbsp of the parsley, and a few grinds of pepper (if using). Stir until a creamy sauce forms. If the pasta is dry, add more of the pasta water. Taste and season with salt, if it needs it.

4. Mound the pasta onto heated plates and sprinkle with the remaining 1 Tbsp parsley and more pepper, if desired. Serve hot.

continued

It's that easy: Bow ties, or farfalle, can cook any-where from 11 to 13 minutes depending on the brand, so check the pasta every minute after 10 minutes to keep track. If you have a small wire-mesh strainer, cook the Brussels sprouts in the strainer, dropping it into the water on top of the pasta. That way you can remove the Brussels sprouts if they cook faster than the pasta.

Extra hungry? The bitterness of frisée is a nice counterpoint to the salty, cheesy sauce on this pasta. Toss a few torn leaves with halved grape tomatoes, thinly sliced cucumbers, a splash of white balsamic vinegar, and a glug of olive oil. Sprinkle with salt and pepper.

In the glass: It all depends on what suits your mood. You could go with a buttery Chardonnay from J. Lohr or Buena Vista, or if you're in the mood for a red, try Caretaker Pinot Noir from Trader Joe's for a steal.

Mac and Smoked Gouda

with SWISS CHARD *and* HORSERADISH CRUMBS

Oh, mac and cheese, how many ways do we love thee? In this rendition, we foster mac's smoky side with smoked Gouda and pique his spicy side with horseradish-laced crunchy saltines. To make things even better, you don't have to boil the pasta. It cooks right in the sauce. Genius.

4 Tbsp [55 g] unsalted butter, plus 1 Tbsp melted	*½ cup [120 ml] half-and-half*
1 onion, minced	*1 tsp Dijon mustard*
1 bunch Swiss chard, tough stems discarded, coarsely chopped	*1½ cups [120 g] shredded smoked Gouda*
Kosher salt and freshly ground black pepper	*1½ cups [360 ml] vegetable broth*
2 Tbsp all-purpose flour	*6 oz [170 g] elbow macaroni*
1 cup [240 ml] milk	*10 saltines, crushed*
	2 tsp prepared horseradish

1. Preheat the oven to 400°F [200°C].

2. Heat a 12-in [30.5-cm] oven-safe skillet over medium-high heat, and melt the 4 Tbsp [55 g] butter. When the butter sizzles, add the onion and sauté until it softens, about 2 minutes. Add the Swiss chard, ½ tsp salt, and a few grinds of pepper and sauté until the chard leaves wilt, about 3 minutes.

3. Add the flour to the pan and cook, stirring, about 1 minute. Add the milk, half-and-half, and mustard and cook, stirring and scraping up any flour that may be stuck to the bottom of the pan, until the sauce thickens, about 3 minutes. Add the Gouda and cook, stirring, until the cheese melts, about 1 minute. Add the vegetable broth and macaroni,

pressing down to make sure the pasta is submerged in the liquid. Cover the pan with aluminum foil or an oven-safe lid, transfer to the oven, and bake until the pasta is tender, about 20 minutes.

4. Meanwhile, in a small bowl, stir together the saltines, horseradish, and 1 Tbsp melted butter.

5. Remove the pasta from the oven, remove the foil, and sprinkle the saltine mixture over the top. Carefully move the oven rack to the second highest position and preheat the broiler. Broil until the topping is browned, about 2 minutes.

continued

6. Scoop the pasta into heated bowls. Serve hot. (Or, if you want it to stay really hot, just place the pan on the table and eat with two forks like my husband and I do.)

It's that easy: It would be so simple to sub out just about any cheese in your fridge for the smoked Gouda. The important thing is that it's good cheese (no low-fat versions need apply). Try using white Cheddar, Gruyère, Jarlsberg, or go ahead and toss some Parmesan in the mix for good measure.

Extra hungry? It's not likely you'll need any more food with this meal, but if you're looking for something to serve on the side, add some crispy, cold dill pickle spears. The sour flavor is a great contrast with the richness of this dish.

In the glass: An off-dry Riesling from Jacob's Creek works perfectly with the rich and smoky cheese.

Shells and Five Cheeses

with TOMATO

When looking for a homey, comfortable, rich, and satisfying dish, look no further. Though there is a tomato in this dish, it does consist largely of cheese (five kinds), pasta, and cream, and what could be bad about that! It is ooey, gooey, and divine with a little (or big) glass of wine and a crust of bread.

½ cup [15 g] grated pecorino romano cheese

½ cup [40 g] shredded fontina cheese

½ cup [40 g] shredded mozzarella cheese

½ cup [60 g] crumbled blue cheese

½ cup [120 g] ricotta cheese

½ cup [40 g] diced tomatoes

¾ cup [180 ml] half-and-half

Leaves from 1 sprig rosemary, chopped

Kosher salt and freshly ground black pepper

8 oz [230 g] small pasta shells

2 Tbsp unsalted butter, melted

¼ cup [15 g] panko bread crumbs

1. Preheat the oven to 450°F [230°C].

2. Fill a 12-in [30.5-cm] oven-safe skillet with water and bring it to a boil over medium-high heat.

3. Meanwhile, in a large bowl, stir together the pecorino, fontina, mozzarella, blue cheese, ricotta, and tomatoes. Add the half-and-half, rosemary, ½ tsp salt, and a few grinds of pepper and stir to combine.

4. When the water boils, add 1 tsp salt along with the pasta and cook at a low boil (lower the heat if you need to) for about 8 minutes. (It's okay that the pasta won't be completely tender because it will continue to soften as it bakes in the oven.) Drain

the pasta and return it to the pan. Add the cheeses and stir until combined. Transfer to the oven and bake, uncovered, until hot and bubbling, about 15 minutes.

5. Meanwhile, in a small bowl, stir together the butter and panko.

6. Remove the pasta from the oven and sprinkle the panko mixture over the top. Carefully move the oven rack to the second highest position and preheat the broiler. Broil until the topping is browned, about 2 minutes.

7. Scoop the pasta onto heated plates. Serve hot.

It's that easy: *I've found many domestic brands of dried pasta become too mushy after the boiling and baking process. For that reason, I like to use imported Italian pasta made from durum flour, which retains a sturdier al dente bite when cooked.*

Extra hungry? *There's a whole lot of pasta in that skillet, but if you need a side, make a salad. Try Boston lettuce, grape tomatoes, and sliced cucumber splashed with sherry vinegar and a glug of olive oil. Season with salt and pepper.*

In the glass: *I can't think of anything but a crisp white to cut through all the cheese. Look for something exciting from South America like a bottle of La Yunta Torrontés.*

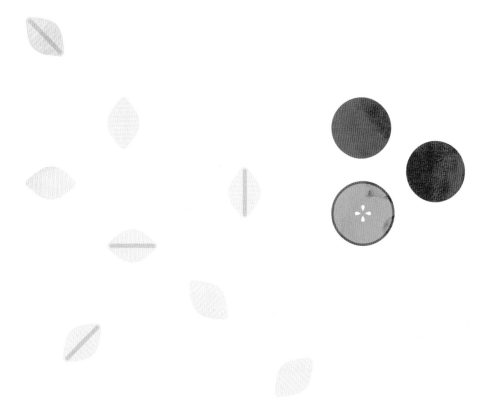

Lo Mein

with SNOW PEAS and PEANUT SAUCE

This is a classic, quick-and-easy one-pot meal. Just toss some noodles, snow peas, bean sprouts, and cilantro with store-bought peanut sauce and sprinkle peanuts on top. It's the perfect ending to a busy workday. Relax—this is another great meal that comes together super-quickly.

Kosher salt

8 oz [230 g] dried lo mein noodles or Italian linguine, broken in half

1 cup [120 g] chopped snow peas

1/2 cup [120 ml] peanut sauce

1 carrot, peeled and shredded with a julienne peeler or grated

1/2 cup [60 g] bean sprouts

Freshly ground black pepper

Chile-garlic sauce for seasoning (optional)

2 Tbsp minced fresh cilantro

1/4 cup [30 g] peanuts, preferably salted

1. In a 3-qt [2.8-L] saucepan over medium-high heat, bring 2 qt [2 L] water to a boil. Add 1 tsp salt and the noodles and cook until al dente (usually a minute or so less than the package directions). To check for doneness, fish out a strand and bite into it. It should still be chewy, just a little underdone.

2. Immediately add the snow peas to the boiling pasta and cook until the snow peas are tender-crisp, about 30 seconds.

3. Reserve 1/4 cup [60 ml] of the cooking water and then drain the pasta and snow peas in a colander in the sink.

4. Return the pasta and snow peas to the hot pan and pour in about half of the pasta water, the peanut sauce, carrot, and bean sprouts. Toss the pasta with two wooden spoons or tongs to completely coat the pasta and vegetables. The pasta will absorb the sauce so add more of the pasta water if it seems dry and sticky. Taste and season with salt and pepper, if it needs it, and chile-garlic sauce, if you like it spicy. Sprinkle with the cilantro and peanuts.

5. Scoop the hot noodles into heated bowls and serve hot.

continued

PASTA FOR DINNER

It's that easy: *One of my favorite things to do with this dish and its kissing cousin, pad thai, is to roll the noodles up in rice-paper wrappers and serve them as a fun eat-with-your-fingers appetizer or picnic dish.*

Extra hungry? *Buy a jar of pickled vegetables, such as carrots, cauliflower, and peppers, and serve them on the side. Their tartness will offset the richness of the peanut sauce, and it's a great way to get your veggie quota in.*

In the glass: *A Chenin Blanc from South Africa is a good choice to pair up with this nutty, spicy dish.*

Gnocchi

with WILD MUSHROOMS *and* EDAMAME

Eating gnocchi (NYOK-kee) in a restaurant is usually hit or miss. The little pasta pillows are either fabulous or terrible, fluffy as a cloud or dense as stone. Take control of your gnocchi cravings and make these tender pillows of deliciousness the next time you need some carbo love. With meaty wild mushrooms and bright green edamame for protein, this dinner looks as good as it tastes.

1 cup [240 g] ricotta cheese	*1 garlic clove, minced*
1 egg yolk	*Leaves from 1 sprig fresh rosemary, chopped*
3/4 cup [25 g] grated Parmesan cheese	*8 oz [230 g] assorted wild mushrooms, sliced*
Pinch of freshly grated nutmeg	*1/4 cup [60 ml] white wine*
Kosher salt and freshly ground black pepper	*2 cups [480 ml] vegetable broth, plus more as needed*
2/3 cup [90 g] all-purpose flour	*1/3 cup [60 g] frozen edamame or peas, thawed*
3 Tbsp unsalted butter	*1/2 lemon*
1 shallot, minced	*1 Tbsp minced fresh flat-leaf parsley*

1. In a large bowl, stir together the ricotta, egg yolk, 1/2 cup [15 g] of the Parmesan, the nutmeg, 1/4 tsp salt, and a few grinds of pepper. Add the flour and quickly stir with a fork just until a soft dough forms. (Be careful not to overmix or your gnocchi will be tough.)

2. Turn the dough out onto a lightly floured work surface. Roll the dough into a log about 30 in [76 cm] long and, with a floured table knife, cut it into 1/2-in [12-mm] gnocchi. Set aside.

continued

3. Heat a 12-in [30.5-cm] skillet over medium-high heat, and melt the butter. When the butter sizzles, add the shallot, garlic, rosemary, and mushrooms. Cook until the mushrooms begin to soften, about 3 minutes. Add the wine and cook until it evaporates, about 1 minute. Add the vegetable broth and edamame and bring to a simmer. Gently drop half the gnocchi into the simmering broth, shaking the pan to submerge them, and simmer until the gnocchi are firm and cooked through, about 3 minutes. With a slotted spoon, transfer the gnocchi to a heated bowl (it's okay if some of the mushrooms escape from the pan with the gnocchi). Cover and keep warm. Repeat with the remaining gnocchi, adding more broth if necessary. When the second batch of gnocchi is done, return all the gnocchi to the pan, stirring them in gently. The liquid should be reduced and thickened to a saucy texture. Add a squeeze of lemon. Taste and season with salt and pepper, if it needs it.

4. Spoon the gnocchi and mushrooms into heated shallow bowls and sprinkle with the remaining Parmesan and the parsley. Serve hot.

It's that easy: "Gnocchi . . . easy?" you may scoff. Yes, I say. Even my husband could roll out this dough; the trick is to keep a light touch. Don't overwork the dough, and stir it only until it comes together. Roll it into a log and cut into pieces. Done.

Extra hungry? Add more edamame. They are packed with protein and very filling.

In the glass: A chilled glass of Iron Horse Chardonnay is my go-to wine with these little dumplings. It's unoaked, so it's lighter on the palate and goes much better with food than more heavily oaked Chardonnays.

....
START TO FINISH
30 minutes
. . .
HANDS-ON TIME
30 minutes
. . .
Serves 2
....

Spinach Gnudi

with CABBAGE and BROWNED BUTTER

Gnudi (NU-dee) are little pillows of indulgent cheesy dough, kind of like ravioli without the pasta covering. When they are browned in butter with cabbage and rosemary, I can actually hear angels sing. As it turns out, it's surprisingly easy to whip up a batch of heaven for dinner.

½ cup [90 g] frozen chopped spinach, thawed and squeezed dry

½ cup [120 g] whole-milk ricotta cheese

½ cup [15 g] grated Parmesan cheese, plus more for sprinkling

1 egg yolk

⅛ tsp freshly grated nutmeg

Kosher salt and freshly ground black pepper

1¼ cups [175 g] all-purpose flour

4 Tbsp [55 g] unsalted butter

Leaves from 3 sprigs rosemary

1 onion, thinly sliced

2 cups [120 g] thinly sliced cabbage

1. Fill a 12-in [30.5-cm] skillet with water and bring it to a boil over high heat.

2. In a medium bowl, stir together the spinach, ricotta, Parmesan, egg yolk, nutmeg, ½ tsp salt, and a few grinds of pepper. Add ½ cup [70 g] of the flour and quickly stir with a fork. The dough should be slightly sticky. Pour the remaining ¾ cup [105 g] flour into a shallow bowl.

3. Scoop the dough with a 1-Tbsp scoop or a tablespoon and drop it into the flour-filled bowl, roll it gently into a ball, and transfer it to a plate. Shape the remaining dough in the same way.

4. Add 1 tsp salt to the boiling water, gently drop in the gnudi, and cook until they float, about 3 minutes. Transfer the gnudi with a slotted spoon to a bowl. Reserve ¼ cup [60 ml] of the cooking water and discard the rest.

5. Return the pan to high heat and add the butter, rosemary, and onion and sauté until the onion begins to soften, about 1 minute. Add the cabbage and sauté, tossing, until softened and the butter has browned, about 4 minutes, and then return the gnudi and reserved cooking water to the pan. Toss gently to coat the gnudi with the butter (be gentle as they are tender and can break apart) and cook until warmed through, about 3 minutes longer.

6. Scoop the gnudi and vegetables onto heated plates and sprinkle with Parmesan. Serve hot.

It's that easy: Using a scoop means you can make all the gnudi the same size without even thinking about it. I like them small, so I use a 1-Tbsp scoop.

Extra hungry? Add more cabbage. You can add another 1 cup [60 g] or so without adding more butter. That is, unless you want to.

In the glass: Ever drink Vermentino? It can be hard to find but is worth the search. A dry white wine grown predominantly in France and Italy, Vermentino is a lighter white that has good acidity and minerality so it partners well with food. Look for a bottle of Mancini Vermentino di Gallura for a good value.

Orzo Pasta Salad

with SUGAR SNAP PEAS, RICOTTA SALATA, *and* TANGERINE

Tangerines are one of winter's bonus points. When they are added to pasta along with salty ricotta salata cheese and crispy snap peas in a light shallotty vinaigrette, this salad becomes a beacon of brightness breaking through the winter haze. Thank you, tangerines. I don't think we could get through the dark days without you.

2 tangerines	*6 oz [170 g] sugar snap peas, trimmed and cut into bite-size pieces*
1 Tbsp white wine vinegar	
1 small shallot, minced	*2 cups [120 g] thinly sliced napa cabbage*
Kosher salt and freshly ground black pepper	*1 cup [140 g] grape tomatoes, halved*
1 tsp honey	*2 green onions, white and green parts, thinly sliced*
¼ cup [60 ml] extra-virgin olive oil	*2 Tbsp minced fresh chives*
1 cup [210 g] orzo pasta	*2 Tbsp minced fresh flat-leaf parsley*
	2 oz [55 g] ricotta salata cheese, cut into small dice

1. In a 3-qt [2.8-L] saucepan over medium-high heat, bring 2 qt [2 L] water to a boil.

2. While the water heats up, zest one of the tangerines. Transfer the zest to a large bowl and add the vinegar, shallot, ¼ tsp salt, and a few grinds of pepper. Let sit for 5 minutes, then whisk in the honey and olive oil. Peel the tangerines and separate the segments. Set aside.

3. Add 1 tsp salt and the orzo to the boiling water and cook for 7 minutes. Add the sugar snap peas and cook for another 1 minute. Check the orzo to make sure it's tender; if not, cook another 1 minute. Drain the pasta and rinse under cold running water to stop the cooking. Transfer to the large bowl with the dressing and toss to coat the orzo with the vinaigrette.

4. Add the tangerines, cabbage, tomatoes, green onions, chives, parsley, and half of the cheese to the bowl and stir to combine. Taste and season with more salt and pepper, if it needs it.

5. Scoop the salad into shallow bowls and sprinkle with the remaining cheese. Serve immediately.

It's that easy: *If you want to be sure to leave your snap peas crispy, place them in a fine-mesh strainer and drop it into the boiling water. That way you can remove them from the boiling water in a minute and still cook the orzo another minute, if it needs it.*

Extra hungry? *How about some cheesy toast? Combine about ⅓ cup [25 g] grated Cheddar, Gruyère, or Jarlsberg cheese with 1 Tbsp or so of mayonnaise. Spread over two pieces of country-style bread and toast in a toaster oven. If you don't have a toaster oven, set your toaster on its side, slide the bread in cheese-side up, and toast. It really works!*

In the glass: *Look for a Soave, Gavi, or verdicchio from the Marche region of Italy. They're food-friendly, fruity, and tart enough to go with most vegetable dishes.*

CHAPTER

6

Pizzas, Tarts, Tartines & Piadinas

START TO FINISH
30 minutes

HANDS-ON TIME
20 minutes

Serves 2

Pizza Margherita

With so few ingredients, a Margherita pizza is a lesson in restraint: it should showcase the best components. Though not traditional, I can't resist slathering the dough with pesto (easily found at the grocery store), which amps up the basil quotient in a much bigger way than a few leaves of basil on top could ever do. Top with vine-ripened tomatoes and fresh mozzarella for a perfect pizza.

1 lb [455 g] fresh or thawed frozen pizza dough

1 Tbsp olive oil

2 garlic cloves, minced

¼ cup [60 ml] basil pesto

2 medium vine-ripened tomatoes, thinly sliced

Kosher salt and freshly ground black pepper

4 oz [115 g] fresh buffalo mozzarella cheese, thinly sliced

¼ cup [8 g] grated Parmesan cheese

1. If you have a pizza stone, place it on the bottom rack of your oven. If you don't have a pizza stone, you can bake the pizza on a sheet pan. (It won't be as crispy on the bottom and may take a few more minutes to bake.) Preheat the oven to 450°F [230°C].

2. On a lightly floured surface, roll out the dough into a 16-in [40.5-cm] circle and place it on a sheet of parchment paper. Transfer the dough and parchment paper to a pizza peel or a sheet pan.

3. Brush the dough with the olive oil and sprinkle the garlic over the top. Spread a thin layer of pesto over the garlic and top it with the tomatoes. Season the tomatoes with salt and pepper and top with the mozzarella and Parmesan.

4. Slide the pizza, still on the parchment, onto the heated pizza stone or transfer the sheet pan to the oven. Bake the pizza until the bottom is crispy and the cheese has browned slightly, about 15 minutes.

5. Slide the peel under the pizza to remove it from the stone or transfer the sheet pan to a work surface and let cool for about 5 minutes before cutting into wedges. Serve hot.

ONE PAN, TWO PLATES: VEGETARIAN SUPPERS

174

It's that easy: *Rolling the pizza dough thinly and then getting it in the oven quickly after topping it will result in a thinner crust. If you allow the dough to sit for even 10 minutes after rolling it out, it will rise higher in the oven, resulting in a more bready pizza. So if you prefer a cracker-like crust, work fast.*

Extra hungry? *The most Italian of pizzas deserves the most Italian of salads to go with it: antipasto. Arrange assorted cheese, pickled and roasted peppers, and olives on a platter and dig in.*

In the glass: *Let's stick with the Italian theme and go with a Chianti Classico or Sangiovese.*

....

START TO FINISH
30 minutes

...

HANDS-ON TIME
20 minutes

...

Serves 2

....

Artichoke Pizza

with PEPPER JACK

I've been making pizza for about thirty years. It started out as a way to save money on my family's pizza night and turned into a better way to eat pizza. I guess we're just picky, but we quickly became hooked on fresher ingredients and how we could make pizzas just the way we liked them. Artichoke pizza is one of my favorites. Blanketed with tart, pickled artichoke hearts and spicy pepper Jack cheese, this pizza can adapt to suit your personal pizza cravings. Goat cheese, blue cheese, or extra garlic? Go for it.

---

1 lb [455 g] fresh or thawed frozen pizza dough

1 Tbsp olive oil

2 garlic cloves, minced

One 12-oz [340-g] jar marinated artichoke hearts, drained and chopped

1 red bell pepper, seeded, deribbed, and thinly sliced

6 oz [170 g] pepper Jack cheese, grated

¼ cup [8 g] grated Parmesan cheese

Kosher salt and freshly ground black pepper

---

1. If you have a pizza stone, place it on the bottom rack of your oven. If you don't have a pizza stone, you can bake the pizza on a sheet pan. (It won't be as crispy on the bottom and may take a few more minutes to bake.) Preheat the oven to 450°F [230°C].

2. On a lightly floured surface, roll out the dough into a 16-in [40.5-cm] circle and place it on a sheet of parchment paper. Transfer the dough and parchment paper to a pizza peel or a sheet pan.

3. Brush the dough with the olive oil and sprinkle the garlic over the top. Top with the artichokes, bell pepper, pepper Jack, Parmesan, a pinch of salt, and a few grinds of pepper.

4. Slide the pizza, still on the parchment, onto the heated pizza stone or transfer the sheet pan to the oven. Bake the pizza until the bottom is crispy and the cheese has browned slightly, about 15 minutes.

5. Slide the peel under the pizza to remove it from the stone or transfer the sheet pan to a work surface and let cool for about 5 minutes before cutting into wedges. Serve hot.

It's that easy: *You can make your own pizza dough, but on weeknights I take a shortcut in the way of bagged pizza dough purchased at the grocery store. Sometimes it's frozen but usually it's thawed and ready to be rolled out, slathered with delicious things, and baked up crispy and hot.*

Extra hungry? *We love pizza and salad at our house. Toss up some arugula with shaved carrot, a squeeze of lemon, a glug of olive oil, and a sprinkling of pistachios.*

In the glass: *The tart flavors of this pizza cry out for a beer. Your fave cold one will pair beautifully, even if it's not Friday night.*

Fig Pizza

with BRIE and ARUGULA

My husband didn't quite know what to think about this pizza and salad combo at first, but after a few bites he totally got it. Crispy pizza with sweet figs, Brie, and a little red onion topped with an herbal salad and a sprinkle of Parmesan is a marvelous play of textures and tastes. We especially like how arugula's bite is perfect against all the cheesy sweetness that lies underneath.

10 dried figs, stemmed and coarsely chopped

1 lb [455 g] fresh or thawed frozen pizza dough

2 Tbsp olive oil

2 garlic cloves, minced

¼ cup [75 g] fig jam

½ small red onion, thinly sliced

4 oz [115 g] Brie cheese, thinly sliced

Kosher salt and freshly ground black pepper

3 cups [60 g] packed baby arugula

1 tsp fresh lemon juice

¼ cup [8 g] grated Parmesan cheese

1. If you have a pizza stone, place it on the bottom rack of your oven. If you don't have a pizza stone, you can bake the pizza on a sheet pan. (It won't be as crispy on the bottom and may take a few more minutes to bake.) Preheat the oven to 450°F [230°C].

2. Soak the figs in 1 cup [240 ml] very hot water until softened, about 10 minutes. Drain.

3. On a lightly floured surface, roll out the dough into a 16-in [40.5-cm] circle and place it on a sheet of parchment paper. Transfer the dough and parchment paper to a pizza peel or a sheet pan.

4. Brush the dough with 1 Tbsp of the olive oil and sprinkle the garlic over the top. Spread a thin layer of jam over the garlic and top it with the figs, onion, Brie, a sprinkle of salt, and a few grinds of pepper.

5. Slide the pizza, still on the parchment, onto the heated pizza stone or transfer the sheet pan to the oven. Bake the pizza until the bottom is crispy and the cheese has browned slightly, about 15 minutes.

continued

6. Meanwhile, in a medium bowl, toss the arugula with the lemon juice, remaining 1 Tbsp olive oil, a sprinkle of salt, and a few grinds of pepper.

7. Slide the peel under the pizza to remove it from the stone or transfer the sheet pan to a work surface, top with the dressed arugula, and sprinkle with the Parmesan. It's nice when the heat from the pizza wilts the arugula a bit, so you can wait a minute or two before cutting it into wedges. Serve hot.

It's that easy: In a perfect world, every oven would host a pizza stone. It would reside on the lowest oven rack, crisping up not only pizza, but the bottoms of pies, tarts, and gratins. Its mass helps to hold the heat and its surface is also a great spot to place braises, stews, and roasts. I never take mine out; it just lives there in my oven 24/7.

Extra hungry? You already have a pizza and a salad but if you're looking for more, toss ½ cup [110 g] white beans with the arugula and dressing before topping the pizza.

In the glass: There's a whole lot of sweet going on here with all the figs, so a sparkler like Gruet brut will make this dinner seem like a party. Let the cares of your day float away on the bubbles.

START TO FINISH
30 minutes
. . .
HANDS-ON TIME
20 minutes
. . .
Serves 2

Whole-Wheat Pizza

with ROASTED CARROTS, ZUCCHINI, *and* MANCHEGO

Roasting these carrots in the oven before putting them on the pizza makes them extra sweet, and the coriander seeds and sage give the pizza a spicy, herbal note that makes it a standout. Though it may seem unusual, you're going to love the Manchego's nuttiness and the olives' saltiness, not to mention the creamy ricotta.

3 carrots, halved lengthwise and cut into 3-in [7.5-cm] sticks	1 tsp fresh lemon juice
3 Tbsp olive oil	1 lb [455 g] fresh or thawed frozen whole-wheat pizza dough
1 tsp coriander seeds, crushed	2 garlic cloves, minced
5 fresh sage leaves, chopped	½ cup [120 g] ricotta cheese
Kosher salt and freshly ground black pepper	8 Kalamata olives, pitted and chopped
One 6-in [15-cm] zucchini, grated	2 oz [55 g] Manchego cheese, grated

1. If you have a pizza stone, place it on the bottom rack of your oven. If you don't have a pizza stone, you can bake the pizza on a sheet pan. (It won't be as crispy on the bottom and may take a few more minutes to bake.) Preheat the oven to 450°F [230°C]. Line a sheet pan with parchment paper.

2. On the prepared sheet pan, toss together the carrots, 1 Tbsp of the olive oil, ½ tsp of the coriander, the sage, a pinch of salt, and a few grinds of pepper. Spread the carrots evenly on the parchment and roast until they are wrinkled and tender, about 15 minutes. Slide the parchment with the carrots off the sheet pan and set aside.

3. Meanwhile, in a small bowl, toss together the zucchini, lemon juice, 1 Tbsp olive oil, a pinch of salt, and a few grinds of pepper. Set aside.

4. On a lightly floured surface, roll out the dough into a 16-in [40.5-cm] circle and place it on a sheet of parchment paper. Transfer the dough and parchment paper to a pizza peel or the sheet pan.

continued

5. Brush the dough with the remaining 1 Tbsp olive oil and sprinkle the garlic over the top. Spread a thin layer of zucchini over the garlic and top it with the carrots. Dollop with tablespoonfuls of ricotta cheese and top with the olives, Manchego, remaining 1/2 tsp coriander, a pinch of salt, and a few grinds of pepper.

6. Slide the pizza, still on the parchment, onto the heated pizza stone or transfer the sheet pan to the oven. Bake the pizza until the bottom is crispy and the cheese has browned slightly, about 10 minutes.

7. Slide the peel under the pizza to remove it from the stone or transfer the sheet pan to a work surface and let cool for about 5 minutes before cutting into wedges. Serve hot.

It's that easy: *If you're looking for a pizza with slightly more nutrition, this is it. We start out with whole-wheat dough, two kinds of vegetables, and cheese, of course. It just wouldn't be pizza without the cheese, now would it?*

Extra hungry? *You should have gotten your fill of veggies, but if it's cold outside, a little hot broth never hurt anyone. Warm up some vegetable broth in the microwave and drink it out of mugs. In warmer weather, try an iced tomato juice on the side, vodka optional.*

In the glass: *The spicy coriander puts me in a Chardonnay frame of mind, maybe something buttery and rich, like a splurge bottle from Rombauer. For a budget-conscious bottle, look for a Chardonnay from Chalone.*

Savory
Winter Squash Tart

with PEAR, LEEK, and BLUE CHEESE

Eating this vegetable tart for dinner is a sinfully rich luxury that anyone can afford. You'll love the pairing of squash, pear, and blue cheese, with a few crunchy hazelnuts thrown in for good measure.

---

12 oz [340 g] winter squash such as butternut, delicata, or Hubbard, peeled, seeded, and cut into ½-in [12-mm] dice

1 ripe pear, peeled, cored, and cut into 1-in [2.5-cm] cubes

1 leek, white part only, cleaned and cut into 1-in [2.5-cm] slices

2 Tbsp olive oil

1 Tbsp brown sugar

½ tsp ground allspice

Leaves from 1 sprig rosemary, chopped

Kosher salt and freshly ground black pepper

1 frozen roll-out piecrust, thawed but chilled

3 oz [85 g] blue cheese, crumbled

1 egg, beaten with a pinch of kosher salt

3 Tbsp chopped hazelnuts

---

1. Place an oven rack in the second lowest position and preheat to 425°F [220°C]. Line a sheet pan with parchment paper.

2. On the prepared sheet pan, combine the squash, pear, leek, olive oil, brown sugar, allspice, rosemary, ¼ tsp salt, and a few grinds of pepper and toss to coat the fruit and vegetables well. Spread the fruit and vegetables evenly and roast until tender and beginning to brown, about 20 minutes. Slide the parchment with the fruit and vegetables off the sheet pan and set aside. Let the pan cool for about 5 minutes, then cover with a new sheet of parchment.

3. Lay out the piecrust on the prepared sheet pan. Sprinkle the blue cheese evenly over the piecrust, leaving a 2-in [5-cm] border uncovered. Top the cheese with the roasted fruit and vegetables. Fold the uncovered border of the pastry over the filling and form a pleated top crust by folding a small section of the dough up and over the filling. Moving to the right, fold another small section of dough up and over the filling so that it overlaps the previous fold. Continue to fold and pleat the dough up and over the filling until the entire tart is pleated. Brush the piecrust with some of the beaten egg evenly and drizzle the remaining egg evenly over the vegetables.

4. Bake until the crust is crisp and golden and the filling is set, about 20 minutes. Sprinkle the hazelnuts over the top and return the tart to the oven. Bake until the hazelnuts are lightly browned, about 5 minutes.

5. Remove the tart from the oven and let cool for about 5 minutes before cutting into wedges. Serve warm or at room temperature.

It's that easy: *My grocery store carries winter squash already peeled, cut into chunks, and ready to go into the oven; and though I wouldn't buy precut onions (they become too strong) or carrots (they look dried out), I think the precut winter squash is a big timesaver. Look for packaged cut vegetables in the produce section. The roll-out piecrust may also be new to you. Once thawed and unrolled, all you have to do is lay it on parchment paper and fill it up.*

Extra hungry? *A salad of baby arugula dressed with a squeeze of lemon, a glug of olive oil, and a sprinkle of salt and pepper would be nice. If you have a little extra blue cheese, feel free to scatter some over the top.*

In the glass: *One of the best buys around is Cline Cashmere Red, a blend of Grenache, Syrah, and Mourvèdre grapes.*

START TO FINISH
55 minutes
. . .
HANDS-ON TIME
10 minutes
. . .
Serves 2
. . . .

Roasted Moroccan Vegetable Tart

with HARISSA

I love how these caramelized veggies with North African heat pair up with the rich goat cheese and flaky, buttery pastry. We loved it for dinner but couldn't stop thinking about how this meal would also make a stand-out appetizer if cut into bite-size pieces. But then we'd have to share with others, wouldn't we?

One 6-in [15-cm] zucchini, halved lengthwise and cut into ¼-in [6-mm] slices

½ small red onion, thinly sliced

½ red bell pepper, seeded, deribbed, and cut into ¼-in [6-mm] strips

1 baby eggplant, cut into ½-in [12-mm] cubes

1 Tbsp olive oil

2 tsp harissa

Kosher salt and freshly ground black pepper

3 oz [85 g] goat cheese, at room temperature

⅓ cup [25 g] grated mozzarella cheese

2 eggs, beaten

1 sheet frozen puff pastry, thawed but chilled

1. Place an oven rack in the second lowest position and preheat to 400°F [200°C]. Line a sheet pan with parchment paper.

2. On the prepared sheet pan, combine the zucchini, onion, bell pepper, and eggplant. Drizzle with the olive oil and harissa, sprinkle with ¼ tsp salt and a few grinds of pepper, and toss to coat the vegetables well. Spread the vegetables evenly and roast until softened and brown around the edges, about 20 minutes. Slide the parchment with the vegetables off the sheet pan and set aside. Let the pan cool for about 5 minutes, then cover with a new sheet of parchment.

3. Meanwhile, in a bowl, stir together the goat cheese, mozzarella, half of the beaten egg, ¼ tsp salt, and a few grinds of pepper. Set aside.

4. On a lightly floured surface, roll out the pastry to a 12-in [30.5-cm] square. Lay out the pastry on the prepared sheet pan. Spread the cheese mixture over the pastry, leaving a 2-in [5-cm] border uncovered. Top the cheese with the roasted vegetables. Fold the uncovered border of the pastry over the filling. Brush the pastry with some of the remaining beaten egg and drizzle any remaining egg evenly over the vegetables.

continued

PIZZAS, TARTS, TARTINES & PIADINAS

5. Bake until the crust is golden brown around the edges and crisp on the bottom, about 25 minutes.

6. Remove the tart from the oven and let cool for about 5 minutes before cutting into squares. Serve warm or at room temperature.

It's that easy: Harissa is a fiery North African chile paste generally containing oil, chiles, garlic, cumin, coriander, caraway, and sometimes a bit of dried mint. It often comes in a can but it's most convenient to buy in a tube. Keep it in the refrigerator after opening or freeze 1-Tbsp-size drops on a sheet pan lined with parchment paper, then transfer to a resealable plastic freezer bag. Now you have a secret ingredient to use whenever you want to zip up the flavor of soups, stews, couscous, lentils, or vegetables.

Extra hungry? Store-bought hummus and carrot sticks are a welcome crunchy, sweet side.

In the glass: An Australian Cabernet Sauvignon from Chalk Hill has the herbaceous notes to stand up to this spicy vegetable tart.

Root Vegetable Tarte Tatin

The French upside-down apple tart, tarte Tatin, is a glory to behold, and this main-course vegetable version is no exception. Root vegetables are so lovely when roasted and caramelized, bringing all their sweetness to the fore. Use a maroon carrot here if you can find it as it adds a beautiful red tinge beside the white parsnip and purple onion.

2 Tbsp olive oil

3 medium new potatoes, unpeeled, cut into ¹/₂-in [12-mm] rounds

1 small sweet potato, peeled and cut into ¹/₂-in [12-mm] rounds

1 parsnip, peeled and cut into ¹/₂-in [12-mm] rounds

1 small red onion, cut into ¹/₂-in [12-mm] slices

1 maroon carrot or regular carrot, cut into ¹/₂-in [12-mm] rounds

Kosher salt and freshly ground black pepper

2 garlic cloves, coarsely chopped

8 fresh sage leaves, chopped

1 Tbsp unsalted butter

1 Tbsp sugar

1 tsp cider vinegar

2 oz [55 g] goat cheese, crumbled

1 sheet frozen puff pastry, thawed but chilled

1. Preheat the oven to 425°F [220°C].

2. Heat a 12-in [30.5-cm] oven-safe skillet over medium-high heat, and add the olive oil. When the oil shimmers, add the new potatoes, sweet potato, parsnip, onion, carrot, ¹/₂ tsp salt, and a few grinds of pepper and toss to coat the vegetables evenly. Cook until the vegetables start to sizzle, about 3 minutes, then transfer the skillet to the oven and roast the vegetables until almost tender, about 15 minutes. Sprinkle the garlic over the top and continue to roast until the vegetables are tender, about 5 minutes longer.

3. Transfer the vegetables to a plate and toss with the sage. Set aside.

continued

4. Let the skillet cool for a few minutes and then add the butter, swirling the pan (careful, the handle's hot) to distribute it evenly over the bottom. Sprinkle the sugar evenly into the bottom of the pan and drizzle with the vinegar. Set the pan over medium heat and place the vegetables back in the pan, arranging them neatly, cut-sides down, pushing them closely together. Sprinkle the goat cheese evenly over the top. Lay the chilled puff pastry over the top of the veggies and cheese. You can trim the corners off of the pastry if you want; just make sure to cover the bulk of the filling, with just a little overlap.

5. Transfer to the oven and bake until the pastry is browned and crisp, about 20 minutes.

6. Remove the pan from the oven, immediately place a serving plate over the top of the tart, flip the pan and plate together (careful, once again, that you don't burn yourself), and turn the tart out onto the plate. The vegetables will be on top and the crust will be on the bottom. Let cool a minute or so and cut into wedges. Serve warm or at room temperature.

It's that easy: *It may sound complex, but it's really easy to pull this dish off. If ever there were a reason to have a cast-iron skillet, it would be to make this dish. There's nothing like cast iron for browning food evenly. You will be amazed at how this tart will just pop right out with no sticking. Honest.*

Extra hungry? *A little salad of escarole, avocado, and sliced grapefruit with a drizzle of white balsamic vinegar and a glug of olive oil offers a refreshing tart to all the sweet veggies.*

In the glass: *A Pinot Noir from Meiomi pairs very well with the flavors of roasted root vegetables, goat cheese, and buttery pastry.*

Spring Tartine

with GUACAMOLE and PICKLED ASPARAGUS

"Tartine" is a fancy, Frenchified word for a type of open-faced sandwich. The word *tartine* (pronounced tar-TEEN) is the diminutive of the French word *tarte* (pie). Once you get the hang of it, you can concoct your own recipes using leftovers and bits and pieces of cheese and vegetables that would otherwise go to waste.

Zest of 1 lemon, plus 2 tsp fresh lemon juice	*15 spears asparagus, trimmed to fit the bread*
1/3 cup [80 ml] cider vinegar	*1 ripe avocado*
3 Tbsp water	*4 slices country-style bread, toasted*
2 Tbsp sugar	*1 small red onion, thinly sliced*
Kosher salt and freshly ground black pepper	*1/2 cup [60 g] crumbled feta cheese*

1. In a shallow bowl large enough for the asparagus to lie flat, stir together the lemon zest, vinegar, water, sugar, 1/4 tsp salt, and a few grinds of pepper. Microwave the mixture until the sugar dissolves, about 2 minutes. Lay the asparagus into the brine and microwave for 2 minutes. Let the asparagus continue to pickle at room temperature.

2. In a bowl, mash the avocado with the lemon juice, a pinch of salt, and a few grinds of pepper.

3. Spread the avocado on the toast. Pat the asparagus dry and lay it decoratively on the avocado. Top with the onion and sprinkle with the feta.

4. Transfer the tartines to plates and eat with your hands (like my husband) or with a knife and fork (like me).

It's that easy: *Buy bread from a local artisan bakery or the bake shop at finer grocery stores. Look for country-style loaves that you can slice yourself. That way the bread stays fresh for a longer period of time. If I'm not going to use the whole loaf, I sometimes slice it all down and then freeze it in a resealable plastic bag so that I can then use it a slice at a time.*

Extra hungry? *Just make another tartine for those hungrier nights.*

In the glass: *A slightly fizzy vinho verde from Portugal sounds about right.*

Summer Tartine

with ROASTED TOMATOES and MOZZARELLA

Nothing says summer like tomatoes and basil with some lovely cheese. You've probably loved this dish as an appetizer on little toasts so why not make it on a larger slice of bread and call it dinner? Many grocery stores sell high-quality basil pesto, so pick some up to keep on hand.

---

3 plum tomatoes, cored, quartered, and seeded

8 Kalamata olives, pitted and coarsely chopped

1 garlic clove, chopped

1 Tbsp olive oil

1 tsp balsamic vinegar

¼ tsp kosher salt

Freshly ground black pepper

¼ cup [60 ml] basil pesto

4 slices country-style bread, toasted

4 oz [115 g] fresh buffalo mozzarella cheese, sliced

---

1. Preheat the oven to 425°F [220°C].

2. On a parchment paper–lined sheet pan, combine the tomatoes, olives, garlic, olive oil, vinegar, salt, and a few grinds of pepper and toss to coat evenly. Spread the tomatoes evenly on the parchment and roast until tender and browned on the edges, about 20 minutes. Transfer to a bowl and let cool slightly. Discard the parchment.

3. Spread the pesto on the toast, arrange on the sheet pan, and top with the cheese. Spoon the tomato mixture evenly over the cheese and bake until the cheese melts, about 5 minutes.

4. Transfer the tartines to plates and eat with your hands (like my husband) or with a knife and fork (like me).

It's that easy: *Buy bread from a local artisan bakery or the bake shop at finer grocery stores. Look for country-style loaves that you can slice yourself. That way the bread stays fresh for a longer period of time. If I'm not going to use the whole loaf, I sometimes slice it all down and then freeze it in a resealable plastic bag so that I can then use it a slice at a time.*

Extra hungry? *Just make another tartine for those hungrier nights.*

In the glass: *A light, red Beaujolais or crisp rosé would be nice.*

....
START TO FINISH
10 minutes
...
HANDS-ON TIME
10 minutes
...
Serves 2
....

Fall Tartine

with PICKLED BEETS, GOAT CHEESE, *and* WALNUTS

This tartine is essentially a salad on toast. Purchased pickled beets and goat cheese liven up escarole, toasted walnuts, and a balsamic vinaigrette to make this your favorite fall dinner on the fly.

---

1 cup [90 g] chopped escarole

1 cup [150 g] diced pickled beets

1 Tbsp olive oil

1 tsp balsamic vinegar, plus more as needed

¼ cup [30 g] chopped toasted walnuts

Kosher salt and freshly ground black pepper

2 oz [55 g] goat cheese, at room temperature

4 slices country-style bread, toasted

---

1. In a medium bowl, toss together the escarole, beets, olive oil, vinegar, walnuts, a pinch of salt, and a few grinds of pepper. Taste and season with more vinegar, salt, or pepper, if it needs it.

2. Spread the goat cheese on the toast and top with the escarole salad.

3. Transfer the tartines to plates and eat with your hands (like my husband) or with a knife and fork (like me).

It's that easy: *Buy bread from a local artisan bakery or the bake shop at finer grocery stores. Look for country-style loaves that you can slice yourself. That way the bread stays fresh for a longer period of time. If I'm not going to use the whole loaf, I sometimes slice it all down and then freeze it in a resealable plastic bag so that I can then use it a slice at a time.*

Extra hungry? *Just make another tartine for those hungrier nights.*

In the glass: *How about a fruity Shiraz from South Africa? A bottle of Que Syrah has a nice ring to it.*

Winter Tartine

with HUMMUS *and* ROASTED CAULIFLOWER SALAD

Roasting cauliflower brings out its sweeter side, and when paired with sour and salty little French cornichon pickles, this tartine topper is a real party in your mouth. The hummus creates a creamy and flavorful layer for the cauliflower salad to stick to, making it much easier to eat with your fingers. Thanks to the Purple Pig's Jimmy Bannos Jr. for the inspiration for this recipe.

¼ head cauliflower, trimmed and cut into small florets

2 Tbsp olive oil

Kosher salt and freshly ground black pepper

3 Tbsp chopped cornichons

2 Tbsp minced fresh flat-leaf parsley

2 tsp fresh lemon juice, plus more as needed

⅓ cup [85 g] hummus

4 slices country-style bread, toasted

1. Preheat the oven to 425°F [220°C].

2. On a parchment paper–lined sheet pan, combine the cauliflower, olive oil, ¼ tsp salt, and a few grinds of pepper and toss to coat evenly. Spread the cauliflower evenly on the parchment and roast until browned and tender, about 20 minutes. Transfer the cauliflower to a bowl and toss with the cornichons, parsley, and lemon juice. Taste and season with more salt, pepper, and lemon juice, if it needs it. Discard the parchment.

3. Spread the hummus on the toast and arrange on the sheet pan. Top with the cauliflower salad and bake until warmed through, about 5 minutes.

4. Transfer the tartines to plates and eat with your hands (like my husband) or with a knife and fork (like me).

It's that easy: *Buy bread from a local artisan bakery or the bake shop at finer grocery stores. Look for country-style loaves that you can slice yourself. That way the bread stays fresh for a longer period of time. If I'm not going to use the whole loaf, I sometimes slice it all down and then freeze it in a resealable plastic bag so that I can then use it a slice at a time.*

Extra hungry? *Just make another tartine for those hungrier nights.*

In the glass: *A buttery, rich Chardonnay from Sonoma-Cutrer will work just fine.*

PIZZAS, TARTS, TARTINES & PIADINAS

Piadina

with ESCAROLE *and* FETA

Piadina are like little Italian flour tortillas, eaten much the same way as a taco. In Italy, piadina are street food and stuffed with just about anything delicious. Escarole makes a hearty filling here, and the creamy feta cheese gives it a Greek twist.

1 cup [140 g] all-purpose flour, plus more as needed

Kosher salt

¼ tsp baking powder

1 Tbsp shortening

⅓ cup [80 ml] milk, warmed in the microwave for 30 seconds, plus more as needed

1 Tbsp olive oil

1 small red onion, thinly sliced

1 garlic clove, minced

Freshly ground black pepper

5 cups [450 g] chopped escarole

1 tsp fresh lemon juice

Pinch of red pepper flakes (optional)

½ cup [60 g] crumbled feta cheese

1. In a large bowl, whisk together the flour, ¼ tsp salt, and baking powder. Add the shortening and blend it into the flour, using a snapping motion with your thumbs and fingers. It's okay if it's still a little lumpy.

2. Make a well in the center of the flour mixture and add the warm milk. Mix with your fingers until the dough comes together. Add a little more flour if it's sticky or a little more milk if it's tough. You want a soft dough.

3. Divide the dough into four pieces and roll each piece into a ball. Invert the bowl, place over the balls, and let rest for 10 minutes.

4. On a lightly floured surface, use a rolling pin to roll out the balls into 7-in [17-cm] rounds.

5. Heat a 12-in [30.5-cm] skillet over medium heat. When the skillet is hot, add one dough round to the pan and cook until the bottom is browned, about 2 minutes. Using a thin-edged spatula, carefully flip the round to brown the second side, another minute or so. Transfer the piadina to a plate and keep warm. Cook the remaining piadina in the same way.

6. Add the olive oil to the hot pan. When the oil shimmers, add the onion and $\frac{1}{4}$ tsp salt and sauté until the onion begins to brown, about 4 minutes. Add the garlic and a few grinds of black pepper, turn the heat to medium-low, and sauté until the onion softens, 2 to 3 minutes. Add the escarole by the handful, letting it wilt before adding more, and cook until the escarole is wilted and hot, another minute or so. Stir in the lemon juice and red pepper flakes (if using). Taste and season with more salt and black pepper, if it needs it.

7. Divide the piadina among plates, top with the greens, and sprinkle with the feta. Fold the piadina like a taco and eat with your hands.

It's that easy: Baking powder keeps these little flatbreads light. The dough is really easy to work with. I have a child's rolling pin that I use when rolling out small things like these. It seems silly, but it works really well. If you don't have a child's rolling pin, a 2-in [5-cm] round section of wooden dowel that's about 7 in [17 cm] long is handy as well.

Extra hungry? Add some canned cannellini beans to the greens and warm them up. You might want to add another 1 tsp or so of fresh lemon juice to brighten it up.

In the glass: A bright and citrusy Sauvignon Blanc from Frog's Leap makes this dinner sing.

....
START TO FINISH
45 minutes
...
HANDS-ON TIME
30 minutes
...
Serves 2
....

Portobello and Beemster Piadina

Portobello mushrooms are the closest thing in the vegetable world to a steak, and when they are nestled in a freshly made flatbread, you won't believe you're eating at home and not in a restaurant. Could it be better than a steak fajita? You decide.

1 cup [140 g] all-purpose flour, plus more as needed

Kosher salt

¹⁄₄ tsp baking powder

1 Tbsp shortening

¹⁄₃ cup [80 ml] milk, warmed in the microwave for 30 seconds, plus more as needed

2 Tbsp olive oil

1 cup [100 g] cleaned sliced leek, white part only

3 portobello mushrooms, stemmed and gills scraped, thinly sliced

1 garlic clove, minced

Freshly ground black pepper

5 oz [140 g] baby spinach

¹⁄₂ lemon

Pinch of cayenne pepper (optional)

2 oz [55 g] Beemster medium-aged cheese, grated

1. In a large bowl, whisk together the flour, ¹⁄₄ tsp salt, and baking powder. Add the shortening and blend it into the flour, using a snapping motion with your thumbs and fingers. It's okay if it's still a little lumpy.

2. Make a well in the center of the flour mixture and add the warm milk. Mix with your fingers until the dough comes together. Add a little more flour if it's sticky or a little more milk if it's tough. You want a nice soft dough.

3. Divide the dough into four pieces and roll each piece into a ball. Invert the bowl, place over the balls, and let rest for 10 minutes.

4. On a lightly floured surface, use a rolling pin to roll out the balls into 7-in [17-cm] rounds.

5. Heat a 12-in [30.5-cm] skillet over medium heat. When the skillet is hot, add one dough round to the pan and cook until the bottom is browned, about 2 minutes. Using a thin-edged spatula, carefully flip the round to brown the second side, another minute or so. Transfer the piadina to a plate and keep warm. Cook the remaining piadina in the same way.

6. Add the olive oil to the hot pan. When the oil shimmers, add the leek and $1/4$ tsp salt and sauté until the leek begins to brown, about 4 minutes. Add the mushrooms, garlic, and a few grinds of black pepper; turn the heat to medium-low; and sauté until the mushrooms soften, about 3 minutes. Add the spinach by the handful, letting it wilt before adding more, and cook until the spinach is wilted and hot, another minute or so. Add a squeeze of lemon juice and the cayenne (if using). Taste and season with salt, black pepper, or lemon juice, if it needs it.

7. Divide the piadina among plates, top with the mushrooms and spinach, and sprinkle with the Beemster. Fold the piadina like a taco and eat with your hands.

It's that easy: Beemster cheeses come from a farmers' co-op in The Netherlands that has been making delicious cheeses for more than a century. They are available at different ages, from three months to more than two years. Any would be fine, but I really like the softer, medium-aged cheeses, as they melt nicely and still have a nice tang.

Extra hungry? Add some canned butter beans to the mushrooms and warm them up. You might want to add another 1 tsp or so of lemon juice to brighten it up.

In the glass: A bright and citrusy Sauvignon Blanc from Geyser Peak.

find it fast

Gluten-Free

- Avgolemono Soup with Greek Salad, 22
- Baked Sweet Potatoes with Black Beans and Spinach, 90
- Bibimbap with Fried Egg, 59
- Butternut Risotto, 122
- Celery Root and Yukon Gold Gratin with Swiss Chard and Gorgonzola, 102
- Crunchy Black Bean Tacos with Corn and Queso Fresco, 139
- Dal Makhani with Crispy Leek, 132
- Eggplant Rollatini, 80
- Eggs Florentine, 56
- Fried Eggplant Stacks with Buffalo Mozzarella, Chermoula, and Pine Nuts, 77
- Fried Quinoa with Kale and Kimchi, 127
- General Tso's Bok Choy with Tofu, 87
- Huevos Rancheros with Black Beans, 64
- Indonesian Fried Rice, 120
- Italian Omelet with Mushroom, Fontina, and Basil, 53
- Italian Vegetables and Fried Polenta Cakes, 72
- Kidney Bean Masala, 37
- Migas, 66
- Moussaka, 75
- Mushrooms with Polenta and Taleggio, 70
- Persian Zucchini Frittata, 46
- Potato Frittata à l'Indienne, 48
- Potato Gratin with Tomato, Olive, and Capers, 97
- Red Quinoa Risotto with Asparagus and Parmesan, 124
- Ricotta Frittata with Spinach, Corn, and Sun-Dried Tomato, 44
- Roasted Brussels Sprouts with Butternut Squash, Apple, and Walnuts, 85
- Shakshuka with New Potatoes, 61
- Spiced Green Lentils with Sweet Potato and Pistachios, 134
- Tortilla Española, 51
- Tuscan White Bean Salad with Sweet Potato and Lemon Vinaigrette, 144
- Vadouvan-Spiced Cabbage with Tofu, 82

Dairy-Free

- Falafel, 137
- Fried Quinoa with Kale and Kimchi, 127
- General Tso's Bok Choy with Tofu, 87
- Indonesian Fried Rice, 120
- Kidney Bean Masala, 37
- Lo Mein with Snow Peas and Peanut Sauce, 163
- Moroccan Chickpea Stew with Harissa and Naan, 34
- Moroccan Freekeh with Butternut Squash and Kohlrabi, 129
- Persian Zucchini Frittata, 46
- Potato Frittata à l'Indienne, 48
- Roasted Brussels Sprouts with Butternut Squash, Apple, and Walnuts, 85
- Sweet Potato Cakes with Apple and Spinach, 92
- Tabbouleh with Pomegranate, 106
- Tortilla Española, 51

Hot Town Summer in the City (summer meals)

- Artichoke Pizza with Pepper Jack, 176
- Avgolemono Soup with Greek Salad, 22
- Baked Sweet Potatoes with Black Beans and Spinach, 90
- Barley Salad with Fennel and Nectarine "Pico de Gallo," 113
- Bibimbap with Fried Egg, 59
- Couscous with Broccolini, Chickpeas, and Fried Halloumi, 108
- Crunchy Black Bean Tacos with Corn and Queso Fresco, 139
- Dal Makhani with Crispy Leek, 132
- Eggs Florentine, 56
- Falafel, 137
- Farro Primavera, 118
- Farro Salad with Fennel, Radicchio, and Pistachios, 116
- Fig Pizza with Brie and Arugula, 179
- Fried Quinoa with Kale and Kimchi, 127
- General Tso's Bok Choy with Tofu, 87
- Huevos Rancheros with Black Beans, 64
- Indonesian Fried Rice, 120
- Italian Omelet with Mushroom, Fontina, and Basil, 53

- Linguine with Ricotta, Zucchini, Sun-Dried Tomato, and Lemon, 150
- Lo Mein with Snow Peas and Peanut Sauce, 163
- Migas, 66
- Orzo Pasta Salad with Sugar Snap Peas, Ricotta Salata, and Tangerine, 170
- Pizza Margherita, 174
- Red Quinoa Risotto with Asparagus and Parmesan, 124
- Spaghetti Cacio e Pepe, 148
- Spiced Green Lentils with Sweet Potato and Pistachios, 134
- Summer Tartine with Roasted Tomatoes and Mozzarella, 193
- Superfood Salad, 111
- Tabbouleh with Pomegranate, 106
- Tortilla Española, 51
- Vadouvan-Spiced Cabbage with Tofu, 82
- Whole-Wheat Pizza with Roasted Carrots, Zucchini, and Manchego, 181

Falling Leaves (autumn meals)

- African Peanut Stew with Braaibroodjie, 32
- Artichoke Pizza with Pepper Jack, 176
- Baked Sweet Potatoes with Black Beans and Spinach, 90
- Barley Salad with Fennel and Nectarine "Pico de Gallo," 113
- Bibimbap with Fried Egg, 59
- Bow Ties with Brussels Sprouts, Gorgonzola, and Hazelnuts, 155
- Butternut Risotto, 122
- Celery Root and Yukon Gold Gratin with Swiss Chard and Gorgonzola, 102
- Cheesy Cream of Cauliflower Soup with Leek and Rye Croutons, 20
- Chunky White Bean Soup with Green Beans and Rosemary-Garlic Croutons, 24
- Corn Chowder and Fried Zucchini Sandwich, 27
- Couscous with Broccolini, Chickpeas, and Fried Halloumi, 108
- Cream of Tomato Bisque with Toasted Cheddar and Apple Sandwich, 18
- Crunchy Black Bean Tacos with Corn and Queso Fresco, 139

Baby It's Cold Outside (winter meals)

Spring Forward (spring meals)

Dinner in 30 minutes or less

index

acknowledgments

Thank you to the extraordinary people at Chronicle Books for creating the most beautiful cook-books in the business. I send much affection and gratitude to my editor Amy Treadwell, for her vision, expert eye, and unerring advice; to managing editor Doug Ogan for polishing the manu-script till it sparkled; and to copy editor Jane Tunks Demel for her tireless attention to detail. *Mille mercis* to art director Alice Chau, designer Cat Grishaver, and photographer Jody Horton, for the gorgeous photography and design resulting in a light-hearted, easy-to-read book to be proud of for many years to come. Kudos to lead production coordinator Tera Kilip and marketing and publicity manager Amy Cleary for putting ink to paper and for packaging and promoting *One Pan, Two Plates* to the masses.

Thanks a bunch to my agent par excellence Amy Collins for making the book-selling process easy. I couldn't have made this book happen without you.

With appreciation to my countless students, friends, and family who've recipe tested and critiqued over the years: Julie Neri, Mary Lohman, Sarah McNally, Brigitte Gottfried, Anne Pitkin, Tammy Karasek, Terri Thompson, Sarina Kinney, Maria Isabella, Anne Gallagher, Elsa de Cardenas, Janet Redman, Mickey Shankland, Kathy Belden, Beth Balzarini, Barb VanBlarcum, John and Kim LaScola, Elaine George, Angela and Terry Gagel, Kelly Ross Brown, Connie Sandberg, Mindy Crouse Artus, Sara Snyder, Lyndsey Snyder, Lynn Baldinger, Sue Gumbart, Maryellen Staab, Jennifer Curley, Mira Narouse, Shalini Makaar, and Dave MacIlvaine. I told you the food would be delish. You guys are the best.

Special thanks to my kids, Jessica, Justin, and Corey; daughters-in-law, Lyndsey and Sara; and son-in-law, JR, for bartending, prepping, cooking, dish washing, and generally entertaining us all at family dinners and get-togethers. And to my beautiful granddaughters, Kyley Sue and Emma Quinn, for making me laugh and keeping me moving. You are my favorite people in the world.

And last but not least, to my loving husband, Rick, who spent many meatless nights at the table, but wholeheartedly embraced eating his way through this book. Thanks for being so easy to feed.